FAMILY-FRIENDLY CHILDCARE

FAMILY-FRIENDLY CHILDCARE

SUSAN KETTMANN

Text copyright © 1994 by Susan Kettmann

First published in the United States of America in 1994 by WRS Publishing, A Division of WRS Group, Inc., 701 N. New Road, Waco, Texas 76710
Book design by Kenneth Turbeville
Jacket Design by Joe James

10 9 8 7 6 5 4 3 2

Library of Congress Catalog Card Number

ISBN 1-56796-041-3

Dedication

To John, Brian and Erica,
who taught me to love children

Table of Contents

**Appendix A: Sample Documents, USDA Guidelines,
Developmental Milestones**

Appendix B: Resources

GETTING STARTED

Entering the world of childcare can be as frightening for you, the parent, as it is for your child. When you enter a childcare program, or interview a caregiver to come into your home, you find yourself in the awkward position of having to judge if someone else is qualified to perform tasks that might still be new to you. In a system where other people are considered the experts, it is no wonder that perfectly intelligent, loving parents might feel awkward and out of place.

This is wrong! You know your child better than anyone else, and only you can provide the base from which a good childcare situation can grow. The goal of this book is to provide you with the knowledge and confidence that will allow you to assume this role and make the best possible childcare choice.

Choosing care for your child is one of the most important decisions you will ever make as a parent, and trial and error methods pose obvious risks. This book proposes a more sensible and organized approach: gain a basic understanding of how the childcare system works, learn to speak the "language" of the childcare system, and undertake visits and interviews that yield solid results. An informed choice, well suited to your child, is the natural consequence of such careful groundwork.

Your child will be changed by the childcare experience and only your careful work can guarantee that these changes will be positive. The information in this book comes from twenty years of experience helping hundreds of parents learn how to locate and identify good childcare. As a family home childcare provider, a childcare center teacher and director, a community college child development instructor, and a local government childcare policy specialist, I have had countless opportunities to assist parents in their searches for childcare solutions.

Unfortunately, childcare is an imperfect system. It has evolved since World War II in response to family needs, but not in any logical manner. It is a hodge-podge of programs and services that serve particular needs and are often unaccountable to anyone in authority. Parents who are loving, caring and concerned frequently make poor childcare choices for their children. This is tragic, because finding good childcare is no great mystery. It is also no mere accident.

By reading through this book at least once, you will gain an immediate comfort level with the subject matter and an overview of the tasks your search is going to entail. Then, as you begin your search, you can refer back to pertinent chapters, using the forms provided to help you collect vital information. Additional resources and readings are listed in the appendices for areas you wish to delve into more fully.

Knowledge truly is power where this task is concerned. If quality care is available, you can find it. And why would you settle for anything less?

UNDERSTANDING THE SYSTEM

Six out of ten American families need childcare and they need it for a variety of reasons. Some work, some volunteer supporting community causes, and some have full or partial responsibility for an aging relative.

Families are changing too. In households with two parents it is becoming increasingly common for both of them to work in order to maintain their standard of living. The number of female-headed households has doubled since 1970 as a result of divorce, separation and women establishing households without marrying, resulting in a further need for out of the home childcare during working hours. Across our nation, about 12 million preschool and 18 million school age children need love and supervision by someone other than their parents for some part of each day.

If you are one of the many parents who need childcare, consider that you are probably approaching one of the most critical parenting tasks that you will ever face. Childcare will change your child and your family, and you will want those changes to be for the better. The only way to ensure positive changes is to choose high quality care for your child, and making that kind of choice is not based on luck. It takes time, commitment and knowledge to find the quality childcare setting that your child deserves.

Thirty years ago mothers rarely worried about childcare. Childcare was affordable, sometimes free, and available everywhere. Most children stayed at home until they entered kindergarten at about age five for their first structured learning experience. If their parents had to be away during the day, care was provided at grandma's house, in a neighbor's back yard, or at a community nursery school.

Childcare was affordable. No one dreamed that

someday families would face childcare costs that rivaled their housing, food and tax bills. If care was needed it was either bartered in exchange for other household goods or services, or it came out of the left over household expense money.

Perhaps most importantly, no one thought of childcare as dangerous. Children were not kidnapped, molested and abused at escalating rates in every city in the country. Newspapers were not full of daily horror stories of child endangerment. Children were the cherished responsibility of the community and the hope for its future. Life was much simpler then.

Enter the 1990s with working moms and dads, and extended families that live hundreds or thousands of miles away. Welcome long commutes, longer days and parents who are stressed all the time, everywhere. It is no longer just mom and dad who put in ten and eleven hours days away from home. Many children literally grow up in the childcare setting, from early infancy until their first day at kindergarten.

Politicians like to kiss babies and talk about children as the future of our nation. Tailgating on children's issues, they make broad promises, but rarely has a unified legislative effort been directed toward helping parents with their legitimate concerns about the way their young children are cared for while they are at work. Except for some subsidized childcare at the state level and the federal Head Start program, little else has been done to nurture our youngest citizens and future leaders, let alone their exhausted parents.

Many parents are surprised to find out that no department or governmental agency oversees or regulates childcare in this country. Do they also know that many of the people who care for children are not well trained and may not even like their profession? And what happens when quality childcare cannot be bought for any price because it is not available?

But there is good news. Thousands of excellent childcare providers offer high quality services and exciting experiences for the children lucky enough to end up in their care. These children did not get there by accident. Their parents cared enough to search carefully and seriously, understanding the tremendous implications of their task. They did not settle for anything less than the best, and with knowledge and determination you will be able to do the same.

Looking for a good childcare match is not a task that can be squeezed haphazardly into a busy schedule as if it were a common household chore. It is a task of paramount importance that should be shared by the caring adults in a child's family. No matter what the realities of your time limitations, you can learn how to use your time to its fullest advantage as you pursue your goal—quality childcare.

Be prepared to ask questions, record feelings and reactions, and visit and observe with a keen and detailed eye. When your search is carried out in a planned way, you can collect the best information available on which to base your decision. You can become a confident, informed childcare consumer so that you can find, evaluate, and choose from the best care in your own community.

What concerns do parents voice most frequently about childcare?

The concerns that parents face with childcare are consistently repeated, crossing geographic, economic, financial and racial lines. Many of these common issues relate directly to the child's age. Parents with several children often are most frustrated when they find they must deliver children at two or more programs to get what they want. Counselors at childcare resource and referral agencies across the nation experience a surge of activity each fall as parents grapple with the cumbersome task of finding separate care for their infants, preschoolers and school age children during the back to school rush. The most common concerns that they hear are:

* finding quality care
* locating care that complements school hours
* finding reliable, safe transportation
* finding care that accommodates work hours
* finding care for children over age ten
* relying on licensing and monitoring by a
    government agency
* finding care that matches the child's interests
* having a smooth adjustment period

What is the difference between childcare, preschool, nursery school, day care and babysitting?

These terms are often used interchangeably, but there are some differences in connotation that you should be aware of before you begin to talk to childcare providers. The term *nursery school* was used primarily in the 1970s to refer to organized group care for preschool children. It has been replaced by the word *preschool,* which is more commonly used today. Using the word preschool also implies that there is a learning component involved in the program. *Day care* and *childcare* are generic terms that encompass the whole phenomenon of caring for young children all day for while their parents are working. Care in this generic sense may or may not include a learning component.

Babysitting is temporary, occasional care by a relative, neighbor or teenager. It would be highly insulting to call a childcare provider a babysitter. Today the peak age for babysitting by teenagers tends to be about twelve or thirteen according to organizations and recreation departments that offer babysitting training classes, so choices in this group are mainly limited to evening care for parental recreational purposes.

Is there any national direction on childcare?

In early 1993, the United States finally joined the other major industrialized nations of the world by adopting the Family and Medical Leave Act. This law allows working parents to balance their work and family roles with the assurance that they can take up to twelve weeks of unpaid, job-protected leave per year to care for a new child or to tend to a seriously ill family member. This is a step in the right direction as it signals a recognition that families are facing serious, new challenges.

Another area in which the United States lags behind is in its lack of minimum guidelines for the safety and health of children in childcare programs. While it is true that even the child development field itself lacks consensus on the issue of just what children should be doing, some leadership from Washington is needed to spur the process on.

A strong movement within the childcare field is

pushing to develop its own systems for assessing and recognizing quality childcare programs regardless of governments stand, or lack thereof. As a result, a number of accreditation programs have been developed which begin to define what quality childcare is for parents.

What role do states play?

Many states are also trying to respond to the needs of children and working families. In fact, every state specifies square footage minimums for indoor play space when young children are cared for. Some are abysmally low; as low as twenty square feet per child as opposed to a recommended thirty-five to fifty feet in accreditation systems.

Most states also set minimum space requirements for outdoor play space as well. Minimum health and safety standards are becoming more common, but over half of all states still do not assure a parent's right to drop in and visit unannounced, whenever they wish. This has been shown to be absolutely necessary for guarding against abusive and dangerous situations of child abuse.

Nearly all states limit the number of children per caregiver in a childcare center, but some of these ratios are frighteningly high. Nineteen states allow a caregiver to care for five babies, while pediatricians and child development specialists argue for a limit of three infants per adult.

One of your first steps in searching for quality childcare will be to find out if your state regulates or licenses childcare providers. Your state department of social services can tell you who, if anyone, is responsible for childcare oversight in your state. When you locate this agency, ask for copies of regulations governing both family home childcare settings and centers, as these might be two different sets of guidelines. Keep in mind that these are absolute minimal standards, not what you can and should demand as you become more proficient in understanding the childcare system. It is extremely important that you completely familiarize yourself with these regulations before making your own decisions on what you will or will not accept for your own child.

Is it difficult to find good childcare?

The supply of childcare is limited by three factors: the physical availability of services; the affordability factor; and the quality. Unless a parent finds all three, an adequate supply is not available from which to choose.

The U.S. Department of Labor statistics suggests that by the mid 1990s about 15 million preschool children will have working mothers. Not all of these children will require out of home care, as family members will care for over half of them. But those that do need childcare will have to compete for slightly over 1 million licensed childcare spaces.

Shortages in both infant and school age care are currently seen in many parts of the country. Care for preschool-age children, two to five years, seems to be in adequate supply in most areas in terms of sheer numbers, but not necessarily in terms of affordability and quality. The best programs generally have long waiting lists.

Why does looking for childcare make parents nervous?

Childcare makes people feel uneasy for a number of reasons. First, parents experience the very real feelings of guilt about leaving a young child in the someone else's care. Guilt feelings accompany nearly every childcare situation, even when the caregiver is a family member. There is nothing unusual about experiencing them and advice for dealing with them will be offered in Chapter 7.

A second upsetting aspect of childcare is fear instilled by the media about potential injury and abuse. You cannot ignore these two considerations but neither should you be immobilized by them. The reality of the situation is not as bleak as the media portrays. Parents who find out more about the childcare system are better equipped to minimize the risks. For every horror story, thousands of heart-warming, positive stories abound about children in safe, nurturing quality care.

How is the safety of children guarded?

No guarantees exist for the absolute safety of your children at childcare, just as there is no guarantee that you can always protect your child from getting hurt at home. However, you can reach reasonable peace of mind as you become more comfortable and familiar with your chosen provider.

Note, however, that no matter how good the situation seems, you should never abdicate your responsibility to act as your child's eyes and ears. Where your child's welfare is concerned, you should never get so comfortable and trusting that you stop monitoring basic safety. This means always taking the time to slow down and talk, visit and listen.

Even if a child is old enough to talk, young children cannot always tell you what is actually going on. They do not always see things objectively, or in the correct sequence. Your daily safety check should include such things as:

1. Listening to what your child finds interesting.
2. Asking the caregiver all questions that come to mind.
3. Talking to other parents to see what they are pleased or concerned about.
4. Volunteering to go on an outing or walk with the children and caregivers once in a while, even if it means taking a day off work.

What are the most important things to look for in childcare?

You should be concerned if you ever feel rushed or pressured into making a choice before you feel ready. You might need to get to work, but saving time with a quick decision can land you right back where you started a few months down the road. If you experience any uncomfortable feelings, no matter how vague, they merit further consideration and exploration.

Quality is a major concern, and should rank above even cost and convenience. All available research says that the major component of quality resides in the person who provides the care. The caregiver is more important than the facility or the equipment. If the staff turnover is high, quality care cannot be achieved.

Finally, your ultimate choice needs to fit your own background and beliefs about caring for children so that your child senses a continuity in the people who are an important part of daily life. Ask yourself these simple

questions to help clarify your own perspective on what is important to you before you even start to look:
1. What kind of experience do I want for my child?
2. What kind of adult personalities am I comfortable with?
3. How much am I willing to alter my lifestyle to pay for care? (This is different than asking how much can you afford.)
4. How far out of my way am I willing to travel?
5. What will it take for me to have "peace of mind"?

What is a childcare philosophy?

Although there is a considerable amount of research about how young children grow, learn and develop, there is no professional consensus about how this knowledge should be translated into programs for young children. Because of this, there are a wide variety of ideas about what is best for children and how they should be spending their childcare hours.

Childcare centers are more likely than homes to have a written philosophy statement available, although a home childcare provider should be able to explain his or her ideas clearly on this subject if a written statement is not available. In some cases, the owner or director has a personal philosophy that is reflected in the programming. In other cases, a program might follow a recognized learning philosophy such as Montessori, High Scope, or Resources for Infant Education (RIE), to name a few.

A program philosophy should be a simple statement that explains what children will be taught and why. In the case of a Montessori program, the philosophy will stress beliefs like individualization and self-discovery. Each philosophy should be clearly stated so that you can understand what your child would be doing within its system of learning. Samples of general childcare philosophies can be found in Appendix A.

In trying to understand and compare philosophies, remember that no single model can suit the needs of all families or children. Many of them reflect valid approaches to helping the young child maximize abilities and development.

How do adult to child ratios affect the behaviors of caregivers and children?

Caregivers and children can interact in a wide variety of ways, ranging from cooperative to chaotic. Some of the factors that can influence behaviors include room arrangement, types and amounts of materials, how materials and play equipment are made available, and the density or number of children in the group.

Evidence conflicts concerning the effect of the overall group size to quality. However, the evidence is firm in pointing to limiting the number of young children any one provider should care for. Childcare staff usually react strongly when group sizes become too large, particularly if they feel they cannot give each child the individual care that is required. The stress of too large a group manifests itself in more crying and fighting among the children, and more critical, detached behavior among staff. This is easy to spot when you visit over-crowded programs.

Does perfect childcare exist?

Perhaps you feel that only you or your spouse can provide the best possible care. You are quite likely right, and therein lies the source of some of your guilt. Non-parental care, by definition, implies at least a different viewpoint, if not a different attitude in the care of the child. Viewed in this way, there probably is no such thing as perfect childcare outside the home.

But, young children are quite responsive to change and can deal well with minor differences between your caregiving style and that of their childcare provider. If there are feelings of love, and if basic physical needs are met, the child will grow and thrive both at home, and during the time spent away from home.

With childcare staff turnover hovering around forty percent to fifty percent nationally, finding quality care is going to be challenging. And even if you find it, there is no guarantee that it will be there for as long as you need it. This makes a careful search process even more critical. While perfect childcare might not exist, quality care does, and with it there are built-in positives. Quality care has been shown to give children a boost in life because of the exposure it allows to classic confidence builders. Activities like learning to change clothes, self-toilet, sort objects, create unique art, and pour liquids tells children that they are worthwhile. Valuable social skills like sharing, negotiating and teamwork offer benefits that last a lifetime.

Does childcare have any built-in negatives?

Even parents who love their children completely cannot deliver perfect care all the time. There are times when crying and arguing are bothersome, and times when dispensing justice gets tiresome. Likewise, childcare must be viewed in realistic terms if you are going to make the system work for you.

For one thing, children in childcare are in groups, a far different setting than that at home, even if siblings are taken into account. Because groups are busy and noisy, children can get overwhelmed from time to time. Tears cannot always be dried and feelings cannot always be soothed. Quiet children can get left behind. Questions are not always answered and concerns are not always addressed.

When children get overwhelmed and are not able to explain their frustrations or ask for help, they cope in ways that can be viewed by adults as uncooperative and disruptive. Unless the caregiver is trained to understand a particular child's needs, the behavior can be labeled as negative. Learning to adjust to group care takes time, and neither caregivers nor parents should expect perfect behavior from a child for the whole day every day. This is something we do not expect even from ourselves!

What is a licensed childcare provider?

In states where childcare is regulated by the state through minimum standards, a governing agency issues a license to providers who have met these standards. The licensing agency provides lists of licensed programs, both homes and centers, to local resource and referral agencies. Among some of the most common licensing requirements found in states are fingerprint checks for previous criminal activities, educational and training requirements, and tuberculosis/health tests.

Unfortunately, licensing does not guarantee staff

competence or program quality. It does not even guarantee that the provider will follow the requirements on a day to day basis. However, it usually guarantees some minimal and important checks into areas affecting your child's health and safety.

Where can parents get help finding childcare?

Finding licensed care is only the first step. Talking to parents of children enrolled in the program, and to adults working there, and checking references carefully remain as your responsibilities.

In the early 1970s federal seed money was allocated to start childcare coordination projects throughout the country in anticipation of federal legislation that never materialized. From this movement, resource and referral agencies developed. One of their major tasks was to develop systems to help parents locate childcare in their communities.

Today a few of these original agencies still remain, but many resource and referral agencies following these early models have developed in communities across the country. The National Association of Child Care Resource and Referral Agencies links these agencies together and can tell you if such a resource exists in your community. Their address and phone number are listed in Appendix B.

Resource and referral agencies help parents to locate childcare, and many also provide support services such as recruitment of new providers, coordination of training, and advocacy for childcare legislation. Their services are generally low cost or free. Most agencies do not provide referrals for persons who come into the home to provide childcare.

Private resource and referral agencies also will help to locate and screen providers for a fee. Some of these handle in-home referrals as well.

What choices do parents have when looking for childcare?

Distinct choices in the kinds of care are available in most communities, each with its own advantages and disadvantages. As you weigh the pros and cons of each you will need to take into account your child's age, personality and previous social experience. Childcare services fall into four main categories:

1. Family home day care — care for a small group of children in the home of the caregiver. In some states they need to be licensed or registered.
2. Childcare center — care for a larger group of children in an institutional setting. May be operated as a public, non-profit or for-profit entity.
3. In-home childcare — care in your home by a non-relative caregiver.
4. Care by a relative — care by a related adult, including spouse, in your home or in the home of the relative.

What are the advantages and disadvantages of each?

Family Home Childcare

A family home childcare program serves a small group of children, generally six to twelve, in the private residence of the caregiver. Many groups include the provider's own children. Depending on the existence of any state requirements, the caregiver might be required to comply with basic health and safety regulations. The fees, hours and rules, and program activities are set by the caregiver.

The quality of a family home day care is influenced by the caregiver's background and basic understanding of children's development and by the ability to individualize the day to each child's interests, abilities, needs and culture.

Advantages:
 * homelike setting
 * small group size
 * mixed ages, can accommodate siblings
 * greater flexibility with operating hours
 * may care for ill children

Disadvantages:
 * not regulated in many states
 * caregivers rarely required to be trained
 * may not include an educational component
 * might not have back-up staff for illness or vacation

Childcare Center

A childcare center is an institutional setting where group care for children is provided. All childcare centers differ in philosophy, total number of children served, funding resources, and type of play environment. Nearly all centers have an educational component as described in their philosophy.

Most states have at least minimal requirements for childcare center operation.

Advantages:
* staff more likely to have formal training
* same-age playmates; socialization
* often licensed for health and safety standards
* has a set philosophy
* often has an educational component
* better access to substitute staff

Disadvantages:
* little flexibility with operating hours
* can have frequent staff turnover
* does not usually care for ill children
* expensive for infants and toddlers
* may require children to be toilet trained
* institutional, non-family setting
* group size tends to be large

In-Home Care

In-home childcare is when someone, other than a relative, comes into your home to care for your child. This person can either live in or out of your home. Other household responsibilities, like cleaning or cooking, are sometimes negotiated. Two families can share an in-home provider so that children have playmates and costs can be managed.

Advantages:
* familiar home setting
* individual attention
* greater flexibility for work schedules
* eliminates morning rush
* eliminates extra commute to childcare
* ill child can be cared for at home

Disadvantages:
* usually the most expensive form of care
* caregiver is not checked or regulated by any governmental agency
* you must check all references
* lack of playmates, unless it is a shared situation

Care by a Relative

Many families feel that only a family member, including the spouse, can give their child the love and attention necessary to proper development. Relatives will often provide care for free or a nominal price, making it doubly attractive.

Advantages:
* a natural interest in the child
* child knows the caregiver
* flexible scheduling usually possible
* free or low cost

Disadvantages:
* disagreements can arise on how the child should be raised
* older relative might not be suited to the task
* lack of playmates
* might be difficult to express concerns with care
* caregiver probably lacks formal training

How can family home childcare providers balance children's needs with those of their own home and family?

In a family home childcare situation your child does not have a caregiver totally devoted just to the care of the children. But if you or your spouse were to stay home with your children, it is doubtful that your day would be so exclusively devoted either.

In the home childcare setting there should be evidence of both priorities, with the major daytime focus being on the children. This takes organization and professionalism on the part of the provider. You can look for signs that children are the major focus by observing the caregiver's sense of organization. Some indications would include:
* a regular, daily flow of activities
* specific, not continual, television viewing
* major household tasks reserved for after care hours
* involving children in simple tasks like folding, table setting, and cooking
* ample play materials in stock
* routines for cleaning up after play

What is a family home childcare network?

The home childcare setting is often preferred by parents

with children under age three because it is more like home. It is also often the only choice available in rural areas. To relieve feelings of isolation, home childcare networks are beginning to appear around the country as caregivers band together to get support and recognition for their services.

Networks offer many advantages. Sometimes family home childcare providers band together for mutual support and professional growth. Their networks can be loose and informal, or incorporated with by-laws and officers. Networks relieve the isolation many home childcare providers feel working home alone. Sometimes a network will contract to provide services exclusively for a particular provider, thereby assuring a steady, uninterrupted income.

Networks are also appearing as community projects to meet the needs of particular groups or neighborhoods. Models in which a group or community plan and build in ongoing funding and resources are proving particularly strong. Local employers, businesses and municipal governments are joining in as cooperative partners in order to enhance the quality of the community lifestyle. Further information on models emerging around the country, or on how to form a cooperative network, can be obtained from the National Council of Jewish Women, listed in Appendix B.

What is an au pair?

An au pair is an in-home caregiver who provides care in exchange for room and board. The idea originated in Europe, and many foreign caregivers come here for cultural exchange and sightseeing. American au pairs are also becoming more common.

A limited time, often one year, is stipulated in the contract. This makes this arrangement largely unsuitable for very young children who need long-term caregiver stability, but there would be obvious advantages for school age children. Names of agencies to contact about getting an au pair are listed in Appendix B.

The social security tax consequences of hiring an in-home caregiver should be carefully discussed with an accountant or tax consultant before an arrangement is made.

What is a nanny?

A nanny is a childcare provider much like an au pair, except from the local community or geographical area rather than from a foreign country. A nanny can act as an independent contractor, or can be hired through an agency. This distinction is critical in determining if you need to pay taxes like social security.

No governmental agency regulates nannies, or other caregivers you might hire to come into your home, so the responsibility for checking references is entirely yours. This is true even if the agency says that this is part of its service.

How do parents find and hire caregivers to come into the home?

Because in-home childcare is not regulated by any governmental agency, you are pretty much on your own in finding someone and checking out their background and references. Agencies that place nannies can be found in the yellow pages of the phone book, or by calling the International Nanny Association listed in Appendix B at the end of this book. The classified sections of local newspapers are another source for finding people in your geographical area, as are local churches and community bulletin boards. All such sources should be used with extreme caution.

If you use an agency, their fees can range from hundreds to thousands of dollars, so be sure you know ahead of time exactly what you are getting for your money. For your own protection and safety, all screening and reference checks should be done by you even if this is included in an agency service.

Needless to say, you will need to check even more diligently if you are locating and interviewing candidates on your own.

If you think that you have located someone who might work, it is a good idea to ask the caregiver to spend a morning or two with you on a trial basis, even if you have to pay extra for this. In this way you can watch for sensitivity to your child and general knowledge of the tasks involved, which is especially important if your child is an infant.

What roles do fathers play in childcare?

Fathers today are enjoying a more active role in caregiving than their fathers did, particularly if their spouses are working. Many report that they are enjoying the role of nurturer even though they may not have had an early role model of their own.

In another new twist, the number of male-headed single parent households is rapidly rising, having doubled since the 1980s. Clearly, fathers are involved in the childcare that their children receive and play an important role in assuring its success for the family as a whole.

First, fathers should be involved in the decision-making process that leads up to the selection of the caregiver. The childcare decision is a major one. What father would delegate away the responsibility for choosing where his child will go to college? And what father would allocate only a few sparse hours to the task? Getting a child off to a good start is the beginning and foundation of all learning experiences. The more involved both parents are, the better the chance of success. And if you are in a single parent situation, a second opinion is still highly recommended as a balance to your own over-involvement with the outcome.

Being involved means visiting final choices, and spending some time talking to the administrator, owner or caregiver. It should also include some time down on the floor with the children seeing exactly what your child will see and experience.

The second area of involvement is ongoing. Most fathers would really like to feel more comfortable in the childcare situation, but in truth they are not always given the tools and invitations that would promote that comfort.

Again, few males will have had role models of males in their own childhood who were comfortable around children and children's activities. This does not mean that fathers cannot learn, and those who are learning do so admirably well. It is becoming a more and more common sight to see a father babbling to a group of infants on the floor, picking up his diaper bag and child, and heading out the door after a fond farewell to the caregiver. In this situation there are many winners, and getting there is well worth the effort.

How can parents identify quality childcare?

Resource and referral agencies can give you the names of childcare providers, but time limitations and liability limit them from telling you which places would be best for your particular child. Fortunately, several new accreditation systems are coming forth from providers themselves across the nation. These processes include both self and peer examinations to validate that the program operates in a manner which assures high quality childcare.

The best known accreditation process for childcare centers at this point is under the direction of the National Academy of Early Childhood Programs, located in Washington, D.C. This rigorous process focuses on an examination of caregiver behaviors and the play environment. At this point, only a handful of centers in any one state are accredited, but the number is growing steadily as the value of the procedure is recognized by both parents and those in the child development field. The cost of the validation process varies with the size of the center, and renewal is required every three years so that quality achieved is assured into the future.

The National Child Care Association has an accreditation process which is also proving useful in identifying quality. Dr. Richard Fiene, who worked on both the NAEYC and NCCA center evaluation processes, found a high correlation between them. The NCCA process has the advantage of being less expensive and shorter in duration. It relies on established state licensing standards from around the country rather than on child development criteria, making it easier to administer. A center with an accreditation from either association sends a strong statement of quality and concern for the children enrolled there.

Family home childcare providers can be accredited through the National Association of Family Child Care. Again, the level of excellence required and the fee for the process has somewhat limited its widespread use to date, but local government and local corporate support of the process is making it more widely used.

The NAFCC process involves direct observation of the program by the provider, a parent in the program and a NAFCC trained validator. Records and procedures for communicating policies to parents are also reviewed. In many communities the cost of the process is being underwritten by local businesses and community organizations who understand the link between quality childcare and a stable and productive community.

What is drop-in childcare?

Drop-in childcare is offered by many homes and centers on a daily, space-available basis to persons who would like to use their services on a non-regular basis. Because the number of children in attendance on any given day is usually below the number of children enrolled, taking in extra children enhances the program income.

Centers devoted exclusively to drop-in care are beginning to appear in some parts of the country. They often advertise as babysitting agencies rather than as childcare, and programming is minimal and should not be considered as preschool. Outdoor play space is rarely available, making long days inadvisable. Many drop-in centers do offer exciting equipment and play activities that have a real appeal to children, who look forward to spending occasional time at them.

Drop-in centers tend to be found near shopping malls and convention centers, and almost always offer extended hours in the evenings and on weekends, making them convenient for parents. If you leave your children at one of these centers, make sure that you can be contacted in the event of an emergency. The use of beepers is common, and is even required in some states.

What is the childcare at bowling alleys and health clubs like?

Childcare provided by the owner of a business is usually not regulated by any agency, so the quality of service depends on the owner's commitment to the service. On the positive side, these programs are free and, because you are nearby, you can drop by and check to be sure that things are up to your standards. They are designed for use while the parent is on site and should never be used to drop off children.

What kind of people work in childcare?

You will find as many personalities working in childcare

as children who entice them to be there. Childcare is not an easy job, nor is it a high paying job or even one that is held in high esteem. It is a personally satisfying career for those who are able to juggle its many demands and duties. A major issue affecting quality childcare is the ability of good caregivers to afford to stay in the profession. The U.S. Department of Labor reports the median annual pay for childcare center work at about $14,000 a year. It should be obvious that those who do not truly enjoy young children do not stay long. Working with groups of young children is exceedingly demanding, and the person who cares for your child is the most important element in attaining quality care.

The kind of person that you are looking for will demonstrate a genuine enjoyment of children and an ability to work with their developing abilities. You should feel free to ask potential caregivers about their background, even in childcare centers where you might feel like the outsider.

If it helps you to feel more comfortable, pretend that the potential caregiver is in your living room and you are interviewing them to care for just your child. Find out how long they have worked in childcare and what are their professional and long-term goals. Ask them what they enjoy most about their job and what distresses them about it. If they cannot think of anything, then they probably are not being honest! Try to get a realistic picture of how they view their job before deciding if they are the right person to care for your child.

A note of caution is in order when discussing caregivers: not all of them are trained in what they do. Not all understand the depth of responsibility that they carry. And not all of them are in the childcare field because they want to be there. For some, childcare is "just a job" until they are ready or able to move on to something more suitable. For others, this is the only "skill" that they feel they have. These non-appropriate caregivers might not be in the majority, but there are many of them working in childcare and you must learn to identify them as quickly as possible. This is why it is so important for you to talk to the actual caregivers, not just to the program administrators or owners.

What kind of men choose childcare as a profession?

Men choose childcare as a profession for many of the same reasons that women do. They are excited about the development of young children, and they believe that they can make a positive impact on that development. A 1977 study of male childcare workers in North Carolina turned up some similar patterns among the men choosing childcare as their career path:

* less interest in getting ahead as compared to men in traditional male occupations
* an altruistic view of their work
* a sincere enjoyment of working with young children
* a desire to contribute something of value to society
* a desire to portray a male role model that is nurturing and warm

The image of the nurturing, caring male might be new to you, but it is an image that is emerging steadily in programs across the country. A male can guide an art project and soothe a hurt feeling just as effectively as a female. An added benefit is the positive role model that they provide for children from female-headed households.

Some of the discomfort with male caregivers stems from the media's portrayal of the male as a sexual abuser of children. If parents carry this image into the childcare setting, it becomes difficult for the caregiver to act in a way appropriate to young children; that is, with physical affection and nurturing behaviors. Physical contact is vitally essential to young children for it is their primary mode of communication and reassurance. Many excellent male caregivers leave their positions because of the unfounded fears that parents convey towards their behaviors.

If you are lucky enough to have a male caregiver, be supportive of this role and person. Of course, valid concerns should always be discussed with the program administrator, whatever the sex of the caregiver, but unfounded concerns should not invalidate and undermine the good work that this person might have to offer to children.

What training do childcare providers have?

Only twenty-seven states require teachers in childcare centers to complete any sort of training, and only eighteen states require a knowledge of first aid. This comes as quite a shock to parents who come to childcare with the preconceived notion that preschool "teachers" receive training similar to that of elementary school teachers. Training required by states to work in a preschool or childcare setting can mean anything from a few hours of classroom instruction provided by the administrator or owner, to actual college-level child development courses. This leaves a great deal of leeway in the backgrounds and abilities of the people who care for young children.

As the link between caregiver training and quality is strengthened through research, and as accreditation programs help to educate both caregivers and parents, it is hoped that national minimum standards will be adopted as to what adults really do need to guide children's development during their critical first years. For now, only your vigilant research into the programs that you inspect can ensure that the right people become the caregivers for your children.

What should caregivers study to prepare for a career with young children?

Early childhood education, or child development, is the formal college discipline that focuses on the development of the young child, from birth to eight years. If your state has an educational requirement for childcare workers, it is hopeful that their required course work is in this area.

Requirements should include basics like overviews of child development, studies of the roles of the family and community in children's lives, the basics of program administration, and curriculum areas like art, music, and language development. Keep in mind that only half of the states have educational requirements for childcare staff and insist that programs include formal training requirements even if they are not mandated to do so.

A national childcare staffing study conducted in 1991 found that almost all childcare workers had some kind of training from either a college, a local training agency, or from their employers. Though this sounds promising, remember that the training most likely includes only a class or two in night school, not a degree specializing in child development. Major efforts in the last few years have gone into defining, assessing and demonstrating quality and its affect on children, both in local colleges and through accreditation processes. Training is a word that is appearing with greater frequency and which should be encouraged and demanded by all parents.

What should children be taught in preschool?

Research is proving conclusively that children have a marvelous capacity to learn when they are young. Even babies are being credited with far greater intelligence and abilities than they were previously thought to possess. In their haste to put these abilities to good use, educators and well-meaning parents have supported the movement of reading and writing down from the first grade curriculum and into the kindergarten classroom. Likewise, it is now common to see preschool children learning to recognize and write numerals and letters of the alphabet. But is sooner really better? And above all, is sooner better for children who enter childcare in infancy and stay in its system until they are school age?

Child development specialists from universities across the nation are warning that sooner is not only not better, but that it might even be damaging and detrimental. Children who are forced to learn in "grown-up" ways (pencil and paper work) before they have time to experience and explore as children are turned off to formal education because they have not been able to experience the joy of learning that comes through discovery and investigation.

Children need time to experiment before they are regimented. Children's art work provides an illustration of the purpose of the freedom to explore. Scribbling is a distinct and necessary part of the developmental process of learning about written language. Between the ages of three and six, children make a natural shift from being scribblers to being writers. In this process they discover that writing carries meaning and they think that adults can read the notes that they make up in their play writing.

Children begin to create their own letters as they learn a few real ones, predominantly from their own names. In time they learn that the letters have prescribed ways of being made. Finally, children begin to ask adults to write down what they say, particularly in reference to their drawings and art work, which are also a means of communication.

A good program will use natural curiosity and ability to move a child forward at an individual pace. They will encourage, but never correct, these early attempts at written language. The concept of writing takes time to unfold, and is more important than the product at this age.

Do children need an academic program to prepare for kindergarten?

A year spent in a quality childcare program will enhance a child's readiness for kindergarten, but not in the ways that you might expect. It is the group experience that is the most valuable learning tool, rather than exposure to academic work and sheets of paper. While it is generally true that the kindergarten of today is the first grade of yesterday, your child still needs the same amount of time before formal schooling to learn about approaches to learning.

Be cautious of programs that promise to give your child a head start, particularly through formal reading or math programs. Given the natural range of learning levels among four-year-old children, it is virtually impossible for an entire group of them to be developmentally ready for such tasks.

Despite a tempting array of preschool learning programs and materials, your child will not get a head start through forced sessions of reading or arithmetic. If the enthusiasm for such activities genuinely comes from the child, worthwhile activities like learning the sounds of letters and copying words will give adequate stimulation.

Research points to age five or six for optimal reading readiness, with an occasional child being ready earlier. One of the best ways to make a naturally curious child dislike school is to force learning and academic tasks too early. If your child is ready to read at four years old, many good books can be found on the market to help encourage such skills at home in a non-threatening way.

In a quality childcare program exciting lessons are

learned, but they have little to do with writing a name or recognizing the letters of the alphabet. These lessons include much more valuable subject matter such as:

* curiosity and love of learning
* familiarity with books
* ability to ask adults for help
* ability to work in a group
* ability to tend to bodily needs
* ability to sit still for short periods
* ability to follow simple, multiple directions
* developing hand muscles strong from scribbling thousands of pages produced with pencils and crayons
* developing large muscles with the ability to run, jump, hop, skip and ride a bicycle

PARENTS AS CONSUMERS

Parents have the same consumer rights in their purchase of childcare service as they do in their purchase of any other service. Unfortunately, childcare is not always looked on as a business, which it must be to survive. Because of the human nature of the service, it can be difficult for parents to accept the fiscal stipulations contained in the contract. Sometimes the very act of making money for taking care of children is questioned.

The emergence of accreditation processes is based on the belief that if parents learn how to identify quality, they will demand it in the marketplace. In reality, it will be years before enough accredited programs are available to really affect the supply.

Quality childcare is not cheap. The adults providing it need to be trained and educated if quality is to become a reality. Unfortunately, many of the people who work in childcare programs are subsidizing the cost of care by accepting low wages and poor benefits. With an average of fourteen years of education, they are among the lowest five percent of all wage earners in the United States.

It is not easy for childcare to attract financial investors because profit margins for a quality program with top management probably peak at about five percent. If caregivers do not subsidize it, and businesses do not invest in it, then the community must find other ways to support its presence. The impact of available, quality childcare on business, education and neighborhoods is very real. The collaboration of all of these key players — business, education and government — is the most promising means of solving the quality childcare issue in individual communities.

Both the provider and the parent need to understand that sound fiscal management is a necessary part of providing quality childcare. This means that conditions must be in place for use of the service and penalties for ignoring these conditions. Conversely, parents can rightly demand that they receive what they have agreed to in the contract.

It is unwise to begin to use a childcare service before a formal written contract is signed, outlining all fiscal and program terms and conditions. This is true for the caregiver you hire out of the newspaper, as well as for the well-known corporate chain, or the neighborhood home childcare program. If your provider does not have a written contract, use the general sample provided in Appendix A.

How long will it take to find childcare?

The amount of time spent finding childcare is probably proportionate to the understanding of the task. If the search is carried out under the illusion that all childcare is pretty much the same, the task will probably be completed quite quickly. One might never dream of buying a car or a home in the same casual manner, and there is no question as to the value of the child over the car.

Your childcare search will take at least several days, if not a week or more. For infant care, a more realistic time frame would be two to three months before the care is actually needed. These are best case estimates, and obviously you will have to work within whatever time-off frame you can arrange, but try to allocate as much time as possible for the task. Most of the search needs to be done during business hours, although telephone screening can be accomplished in the early morning and late afternoon hours if necessary. Unfortunately, those are two busy times in the childcare day and it could take you longer to get calls returned and questions answered.

Plan to spend at least some daytime (preferable morning) hours when you are ready to visit programs. If both parents can help with the search, so much the better. Making your final decision might be easy, but in other cases the choice might not be so clear. If you are lucky enough to end up with two good choices, and you feel pressured about making a decision, it might be worth paying two non-refundable deposits while you take a little more time to make another visit and decide.

How much does childcare cost?

Childcare is an expensive budget item which ranks right along with food, shelter and taxes as a major household expenditure. For families with two or more children, the childcare bill can easily negate the benefit of being a two-paycheck family. The good news is that your childcare costs decrease as your child gets older and needs less individual care. Parents of infants and toddlers often work just to protect their seniority and job security, knowing that eventually their childcare bills will consume less of their take-home pay.

Infant care (birth to two years) is the most expensive childcare service, ranging anywhere from about $75 to $200 a week, depending on the supply and geographic location. Preschool care averages from about $60 to $125 per week, and is roughly the same in either home or center settings. School age programs are slightly more expensive in center settings, but rarely is a choice available due to the limited number of programs for children of this age. The price will vary depending on the school schedule, with summer or off-track (for year-round schools) schedules being higher, and hourly fees averaging $2 to $3 per hour.

Is cost related to quality?

The amount of money that you pay for childcare does not always have a direct correlation to what you get in return. Think of it in terms of selecting a restaurant. Some expensive restaurants are worth every penny you spend, and other expensive restaurants leave you feeling cheated. Likewise, there are inexpensive restaurants that are consistently enjoyable, and inexpensive restaurants that serve mediocre or poor-quality food along with their lower prices.

What this means is that you might not have to pay the highest going rate to get quality childcare. On the other hand, you need to be cautious of prices that are too low, for quality childcare does require minimal resources. If you are getting a favorable tuition rate because your child will be lacking basic supplies and materials, or because the caregiver makes a minimum wage, you have not found a good solution to the affordability issue.

One good way to decide how much you can pay for childcare is to compare it to your other bills and prioritize it in terms of your other expenses and the material items that you want. Calculate how much you will be paying for the next couple of years for childcare and balance that knowledge with other material items you might want to purchase during that time period. If you are going to need a new car, the trade-off for quality childcare might be getting a second-hand car for the next three years, or buying a basic, rather than a "loaded" model. Likewise, you need to decide if a local summer vacation is in order for a few years so that your childcare tuition increases can be covered. It is fairly common for rates to increase at a rate of 3 percent to 5 percent per year.

Finding someone who is $10 a week cheaper so that you can afford to fund another priority is a decision that only you and your family can make. Hopefully, you will be able to take a realistic look at the cost of good childcare and will be willing to make lifestyle modifications for a few years that will allow you to meet that obligation more comfortably.

A local resource and referral agency can give you valuable information about current market rates among the childcare programs in your area before you begin your search. This might spare you from being too shocked when you actually begin to make your inquiry calls.

Can parents get help paying for childcare?

Depending on economic, income and employment status, a variety of federal, state and local funds are available to parents. These programs primarily serve parents who are in job training or educational programs, or who become eligible by their income level. Many of the childcare programs where this funding can be used also provide peripheral services like medical and dental screenings, housing and food assistance and counseling. Unfortunately, there are usually waiting lists for childcare subsidies. A resource and referral agency can direct you to any funds for which you might qualify and can help you to get onto waiting lists.

For parents trapped in the middle-income brackets there are no direct subsidy monies available unless the employer offers them as a benefit. However, tax benefits may offer some relief. One is the federal Child Care Tax Credit, which allows working parents to claim a percentage of actual childcare costs as a credit against federal income taxes owed. Naturally, the credit amount will vary with the family income and tax liability. The federal Earned Income Tax Credit is another form of assistance for working families with incomes at or below about $20,000. By claiming this credit, a parent receives a refund for a percentage of childcare expenses paid out during the year. Some states offer similar credits against your state tax liability. You can get information and required forms from your state franchise tax board and the IRS.

One of the most useful benefits currently being offered by employers to help their workers pay for childcare is the Dependent Care Assistance Plan, also known as the DCAP. About sixty percent of large companies offer DCAPs. The plans operate under IRS code and allow parents to set aside pre-tax dollars to pay for up to $5,000 a year of their childcare expenses, significantly reducing their annual childcare expense. If the DCAP is used, the federal Child Care Tax Credit cannot be used. If the family income is over $25,000 per year, the DCAP usually saves more. Any tax service or accountant can review your previous years taxes and help you decide how you can cut your childcare expenses most efficiently through the use of these tax benefits.

What should a contract contain?

Written contracts are common in both centers and home childcare programs. You should also use one if you hire anyone to come into your home to provide childcare services. A model for a general purpose contract can be found in Appendix A.

A contract with your provider protects your right as a consumer. Although you might not like to think of childcare as a business, you need to understand that it is an agreement between two parties for the purchase of services, and that both parties have rights and responsibilities.

The contract should be executed at the time you enroll your child in the program. It should outline rules and limitations clearly, eliminating later misunderstandings or arbitrary treatment. The provider should outline all financial aspects of the enrollment of your child, as well as rules for such areas as the following:

* enrollment and withdrawal procedures
* hours
* vacation days
* eating arrangements
* clothing and supplies
* illness and medication
* miscellaneous; ie. discipline, philosophy, nap policy

You can negotiate to add items for any individual needs and special circumstances you might have. It is best if you can anticipate any such special needs before they happen so they are in the contract when you need them.

Is a contract legally binding?

A contract does not have to be notarized or written in legal language to be legally binding. As long as there is mutual agreement and an exchange of some commodity, fees in this case, it is legally binding to both parties. Rules or attachments that are referred to in the contract language are also legally binding.

Under what circumstances can a contract be changed?

A contract can be changed any time that there is mutual consent, but verbal agreements reached during a discussion are not binding unless added to the contract. The provider can change the contract, provided that you are given sufficient notice of any changes that are to be made. A tuition change is a common example of a contract change. If you do not wish to sign such a change, you are free to leave and change providers at that time, complying with any notice requirements for leaving that you agreed to in the beginning.

What does the basic fee cover?

Unless your contract states differently, your tuition fee covers all of the basic services that your child will be receiving. Be sure to check language carefully, asking for any clarification that is necessary. In many cases this will be the first time that you have ever seen a childcare contract, so it is natural that you will have concerns and questions. Do not be embarrassed about needing to ask about anything contained in the contract.

The basic tuition that you pay is budgeted to cover staff salaries and benefits, rent and utilities, and consumable items like paper, crayons and food. Beyond that, very little remains for field trips, new equipment, repairs and enrichment classes. These items are sometimes covered through additional fees and fundraisers, which you will undoubtedly be asked to support. Candy sales and flea markets have become a regular part of most childcare center programs, although home childcare providers generally shy away from such activities.

Additional fees might be charged for meals, although a morning and afternoon snack are often included in the basic tuition rate. In some states the snacks and lunch are required for licensing.

Is there a charge for days when a child is absent?

Absence policies vary, but most programs expect you to pay the full contracted rate regardless of whether or not your child is in attendance. The childcare budget is based on the number of children enrolled, with staff and operational costs remaining constant. Because there is so little leeway in a childcare budget, most programs could not manage to remain consistent in their quality if they were uncertain of their income from day to day. Some programs do allow for a set number of absence days per year either for vacations or for illness, but this is becoming less and less common. In either case, this policy should be clearly addressed in the contract as it is one of the most controversial of all childcare policies.

Occasionally, under special circumstances not outlined in the contract, fees will temporarily be altered for the parent's benefit. One example of this is when a chickenpox outbreak occurs. If a large proportion of the children are absent and parents are having to pay for a babysitter in the home, special arrangements are sometimes made for a reduced temporary rate to help the parents deal with the situation. To do this, the provider might have to temporarily "lay off" some of the staff, and this can often be done on a voluntary basis. If something like this is done it is probably a good will effort on the part of your provider, taken at some personal loss and should be graciously acknowledged.

Where do childcare dollars go?

If you multiply the number of children running around a childcare program by the weekly tuition, the result is a fairly impressive figure. Unfortunately for most owners and staff, the money is not going into their pockets. Fifty percent to 90 percent of the income goes to staff salaries and benefits, yet childcare is still one of the lowest paid professions in the country. Many owners or directors will share expense figures with you. In fact, many of them would be delighted to have someone interested enough to go over them. If a program is offering high quality childcare, the provider has nothing to hide in the way of financial windfalls. Larger childcare chains, particularly those that operate for a profit, might be less willing to do so, but should be able to give you a general idea of how their income is used for expenses.

If meals are included, what kinds of a foods should be served?

If food is served, weekly menus should be posted for parents to view ahead of time. This is especially important for children with food allergies or any intense food dislikes. In either of these cases it is wise to find out if a meal can be sent from home or if the program will provide an alternate dish.

It is also a wise idea to post menus as children are not always reliable reporters of what was served for lunch. A parent once came to me to complain that we served carrot soup for lunch every day. The source of his information was his three-year-old son who went to great lengths every evening to complain about the cruelty. The father was surprised to read our menu and discover that we never served carrot soup!

Are there mealtime rules for children to follow?

Mealtimes provide wonderful opportunities for children to learn basic nutrition. A menu low in sugar and fats, with low-fat milk, will model lifelong healthy eating patterns. Children receive their minimum daily nutritional allowances in a program that serves breakfast and lunch following the USDA guidelines. These guidelines are outlined in Appendix A, or you can mail for a copy using the USDA address in Appendix B.

Another added benefit to group meals is that the adults can model social eating behavior, and children can experience the pleasure of sharing food in a relaxed and pleasant environment. Mealtimes offer opportunities for cultural awareness. Every child should see the kinds of foods served at home on the childcare menu, from time to time.

Adults should sit and eat with children, rather than running around serving and wiping up spills. Group meals can also be used to demonstrate the fun of trying new foods. It amazes parents to see their children eating foods they would always refuse at home.

What kinds of snacks are appropriate?

Young children get hungry between meals because most cannot eat enough at one setting to satisfy them until the next meal. Their stomachs are small and they burn up a large amount of calories in their play. Normally a snack is served mid-morning and in the afternoon after the rest period. In some states these snacks are mandated, as well as their contents.

Because snacks play an important role in young children's diets, it is important that they be nutritious. Junk and processed foods have no place in childcare, and convenience foods should be limited due to high salt and fat content. Fresh fruit and vegetables, cheese, yogurt, Graham crackers and unsweetened cereals are good choices. A nutritious sample snack menu is provided in Appendix A so that you can see what the USDA guidelines recommend.

HOW CHILDCARE WORKS

Childcare centers can range in size from twelve to more than two-hundred children. Facilities include new buildings designed specifically for childcare, and converted and remodeled space in churches, schools, old homes and shopping centers.

Centers operate for a variety of reasons; to make a profit, to further a religious or community cause, and to fulfill someone's personal dream. Why a program operates is an important item to know when beginning to compare, contrast and reach a childcare decision. Following is a short synopsis of some of the major operational types of childcare centers.

Non-Profit

Childcare centers had their beginnings in non-profit settings during World War II in response to the need for women to work in the factories. Today, childcare centers are still found in the non-profit sector in response to the social needs of children and families.

A non-profit childcare center has a board of directors which often includes some community leaders and other notable professionals. Many non-profit centers operate with a combination of public and private funding, and fundraising is common. Non-profit centers do not necessarily serve just low income families. Many are set up to serve working parents within the community as well.

Mom and Pop Centers

Small centers, also known as "mom and pop" programs, are often family owned and operated. As small businesses, they can yield a modest profit margin if they are carefully operated, and if the family provides much of the support services (gardening, cleaning, etc).

The owners usually create a childcare philosophy and setting directly reflecting their personal philosophies about how children learn. One of the best ways to evaluate these programs is to ask the director to describe these beliefs about young children.

Mom and pop centers are disappearing in many communities just like the corner grocery store and the family restaurant. Little formal research has been conducted on mom and pop centers, and the quality that they deliver varies widely. On the positive side, these programs are highly individualized, reflecting the personalities and attitudes of their owners.

Corporate Chains

The movement towards corporate childcare chains began in earnest in the 1970s. Chains flourished because they were better able to cope with inflation and increased operational costs through bulk purchasing and tax structure benefits. Corporate childcare centers are found mainly in suburban areas, where working, middle income families live and work. They can be recognized by their stylized buildings and standardized programming methods.

Corporate chains like to stress the uniformity in their programs. They claim that a child enrolled in their program can move to another of their sites and experience continuity in their childcare. These claims of uniformity may or may not be true. In terms of play materials, program content and building arrangement there are definite similarities, but quality can vary considerably from center to center due to differences in staffing. Ultimately, as with any childcare program, it is the staff and the director, not the corporation, that ultimately sets the tone of the program.

The question of the appropriateness of profit-making in childcare is continually brought up in any discussion of corporate chains. Shareholders expect a return, and critics argue that profit is provided at the expense of staff salaries. In fairness, corporate chains are not the only childcare programs trying to make a profit, and quality or lack thereof, cannot be directly tied to the profit motive. Corporate childcare is a direct answer to the need to control the costs inherent in the service, and the task of looking closely and at each individual center still remains for the parent.

Employer-Sponsored Centers

Since the 1980s many corporations and businesses have begun to recognize the impact of the childcare situation on worker productivity. One way of addressing the issue has been the construction and support of child employee-care centers.

Some outstanding models of quality employer-sponsored programs are currently in operation around the country. They stress on high quality programming because their company name is linked to the program, and because their liability is greatly limited by their adherence to the highest standards. Major injury lawsuits are unheard of in employer-sponsored childcare centers, demonstrating that the careful planning and execution of quality childcare can indeed pay off. A list of some of these exemplary corporate programs can be found in Appendix B.

Who manages a childcare center on a daily basis?

A childcare center is administered by a director. In some cases the director might also be the owner. A large center (seventy-five or more children) might have an assistant director as well, to help with fee collection, bookkeeping, and other duties in the director's absence.

A center director should have a solid academic background in Early Childhood Education/Child Development, and experience working with young children in a group care setting. If your state licenses childcare, you can check the state childcare guidelines to find out what the minimum director requirements are in your area. These requirements are minimal, and a quality program should have a director whose background exceeds such standards.

What are the director's responsibilities?

Directors are busy people whose job encompasses far more than a knowledge of child development. Some of the additional responsibilities include any or all of the following:

General:
* compliance with local and state regulations
* administrative duties
* staff and child records
* program tours
* communication with parents
* attendance reports
* knowledge of current research
* supervision and knowledge of all classroom activities

Fiscal:
* fiscal reports
* annual budget
* monthly operating budget
* supply budget and purchase
* supply distribution
* equipment maintenance
* inventory
* enrollment
* fee collection

Staff:
* staff training
* staff records
* substitutes
* staff meetings
* staff problems

Community:
* welcome visitors
* community events
* community service projects
* awareness of state and national legislation

Does a family home childcare have a similar person in charge?

By definition, a family childcare home operates out of the residence of the adult who provides the service. This person is referred to as the caregiver, operator or provider. This person works alone if the group of children is small, or with an adult helper more than eighteen years old if the group is larger. Definition of large or small groups might be specified by existing state regulations. If no state regulations for a home childcare group size are available, the consensus of child development professionals on a quality group size would be four to six for a small group, and seven to twelve for a large group, which requires more than one adult.

The home childcare provider puts in long days, often twelve or more hours, with shopping and family chores taking place on their own time. The provider plans all activities, sets all policies and handles all fiscal matters. Consider these ongoing duties when setting up an appointment with a home childcare provider, particularly if you want undivided attention. And when you are visiting, you should never see children left unattended or crying while the provider is talking with you or another parent.

Aren't individual home childcare providers isolated?

Without a doubt, home childcare providers do experience a great deal of isolation in their job. This one factor causes many of home providers to give up their occupation after an average of about two years. To relieve the stress of long hours and professional isolation, groups of home childcare providers are beginning to join together to form local networks. Depending on the level of organization within these networks, new benefits like credit union membership, group insurance, and training are being instituted for the members' benefit. Networks lend a more professional image to the participating providers who dislike being thought of as little more than babysitters. You can find out about networks in your area from a resource and referral agency or by looking in the yellow pages in the childcare section.

What is a typical day in childcare like?

Regardless of the type of care that you choose, the day should follow a basic outline or plan. Samples of general daily plans for childcare centers and childcare homes can be found in Appendix A. Someone hired to come into your home should also sit down with you and develop a similar schedule so that your child will have the predictability that is necessary for learning and development, and so that you can feel confident there is consistency within your home.

Young children need the structure provided by fairly regular times and sequences of events on a day-to-day basis. Predictability provides them with a comfort level that enables them to better cope with separation and lengthy absences of their parents. Even infants learn quickly to predict when the parent is due to return because of the predictability of the day. They will begin to fuss, as if on cue, a few minutes before their parent's expected return time.

Daily activities should demonstrate a balance of quiet and active times, of time spent alone and time spent with others, of indoor and outdoor play, and of both planned and spontaneous activities.

Is separation from the parent typically a problem?

Going into a group childcare setting places a set of demands and expectations on your child that are likely to be totally unfamiliar. Even good routines followed at home are only minimally helpful in making adjustments to childcare. Consider some of the first experiences that the young child is likely to encounter at childcare:

* talking to adults as a member of a group, rather than as the only individual
* competing, sometimes intensely, for the adult's attention
* having toys and play equipment allocated out through a whole group
* waiting and taking turns for everything
* minding "codes" of behavior and manners

It can take days, or even weeks, for a child to figure out what is expected and what responses will be most effective. There is also the added fear of being alone and of wondering if the parent will come back. Adjusting to so many changes simultaneously means that the child must become more independent. While that is a worthwhile goal, it is not an easy or quick one for the young child to achieve.

Being honest with your own ambivalent feelings will help you to allow your child to do the same. Accepting his or her unique and individual reactions, and then allowing for the necessary transition time to modify them, is part of the childcare task that every parent and child faces. Praising your child for acting brave and grown-up could actually cause more stress if the child feels that this posture has to be maintained all of the time. Make sure your child knows that it is acceptable to feel scared or apprehensive. Manipulation is an even less effective coping technique, but one that most parents at least consider. Bribing a child with a sugary treat for "good" behavior might help the child deal with the immediate moment, but it does not even begin to address the real issues. The worst technique of all involves sneaking out once the child has settled down and become involved in an activity. This is a way of directly lying to the child which can undermine all the progress a child has made in accepting and adjusting to the new situation.

A few of the more productive strategies you can try include beginning with a gradual starting schedule and staying with your child for decreasing periods of time, and reading books to the child that talk about the feelings involved in separation and starting childcare.

How do caregivers get groups of children to do things together?

A well-trained caregiver works effectively with children both in groups and individually, and understands the role of both kinds of interactions. If the group is large, activities like eating and toileting need to be done together and in a fairly structured way. Children learn these routines and handle them quite well, even feeling a sense of accomplishment for their ability to perform like the other children in the group. Parents are amazed to see an adult getting twelve children fed, when they have difficulty getting just one to the table.

How much time should be spent playing, and how much learning?

All parents want to give their children the best preparation possible for elementary school learning. They want their child to have every possible advantage, but they do not always know the best way to assure this advantage. A high quality program helps parents to understand how young children learn and the critical role of play in their learning process.

Unlike their older elementary school counterparts,

preschool children do not learn by sitting at a table with a paper and pencil. They learn by touching, feeling and handling a variety of interesting materials. They use their fingers, toes, eyes, ears and mouths to investigate and understand weight, balance, number, color and sequence.

Play is the work of young children. It is the basis of all their learning and it is the basis of any quality childcare program. By coloring, cutting and pasting, children strengthen their immature hand muscles, making them ready for the later paper tasks in kindergarten. Most research points to age five or six as the optimal time for reading and writing. Before children are physically able to write, they grasp writing tools rigidly and uncomfortably. They need several years of free exploration and experience with writing tools before their hand muscles are ready for the task.

Pretend play is another valuable preschool activity. It can begin as early as eighteen months and should continue into adulthood. It is a type of play in which symbols are used to represent objects and ideas that are not present. Thus, blocks become birthday cakes and a line of chairs becomes a train. Pretend play directly affects the child's development of literacy. The emerging ability to use explicit language to negotiate multiple pretend roles and hypothetical situations is the same process that will allow the older child to compose a story. Thinking and problem solving are enhanced as children play through their ideas by using a variety of alternatives to solve imaginary problems.

As you search for a program to help prepare your child for later school success, keep in mind that this is the only time in your child's life when play will be allowed as the prime learning vehicle. Play helps your child to develop social skills, creativity and concentration. Children grow intellectually and emotionally if they are allowed to spend their early years in just this way.

What role does art play in a quality program?

Art is one of the main avenues through which young children learn about written language and creativity — two very worthwhile goals. It takes all of the preschool years and thousands of scribbles and art projects to strengthen hand muscles so that they are finally ready to approach the task of writing.

What might look like random marks to you are actually parts of progressive stages of markings that a child will do naturally if given the proper tools. Thus, the toddler begins by scribbling horizontal lines, followed by vertical lines a bit later. Circles appear between ages two and three, and by age four, the child will draw two lines that cross or intersect, termed a "mandala". The crossed lines then emerge in pictures as designs, boxes and radiant suns. Pictures are the first story-telling language that children create. Soon after, they ask adults to write and read back words on their pictures to tell about their stories. In imitation of this adult skill, children attempt to make their own letters, and writing begins. Left to their own devices, children all over the world follow this sequence.

Creativity is also discovered through preschool art endeavors as the child experiments with color, texture and individuality in the process and the product. All children are innately creative, although most of them sadly begin to lose this wonderful ability when formal schooling begins.

Art that is precut, or in which the child must create something that looks like a "model", contributes little to the child's creative abilities. It is also a source of frustration as the child recognizes that the end product is not as tidy or attractive as the model. Many young children experience this same frustration when they are given a page from a color book and they know that it is a sign of failure to go "outside" the lines.

All caregivers should proudly and prominently display the creative art work that children produce. Creative art work validates the child's uniqueness and diversity, and should be used to decorate the environment in the same way that you decorate your home with objects that you treasure and which reflect you.

What about "messy" play?

If you have an out-of-home childcare provider, messy art and play will relieve you from having to cope with the mess! After all, what more could a parent want than clay, paint and mud on someone else's floor?

Messy creative art projects excite most children, and they belong in the preschool curriculum. Water, mud and fingerpaint feel good to the child's emerging sense of touch and allow the hands to act with both intent and impulse. The process also has a therapeutic and calming effect on troubled, upset children. A tub of sudsy water with some dishes or toys to wash will calm even the most out-of-control child.

If you are concerned about damage to clothing, send play clothes to childcare that are specifically designed for active, messy play. Let your caregiver and your child know that it is all right to get dirty. A spotless child at the end of the day should probably be cause for some concern!

What are educational toys?

Programs use this term with an authority that can make you feel baffled and confused. In the simplest sense, the word "educational" means a material that a child can use without adult assistance. An example is an infant toy in which the child pushes a button and something pops up. The child learns the correlation between pushing the button and making the figure pop up without having to be shown.

What many consumers do not realize is that "educational" does not necessarily mean fun or inviting. The young child continually seeks novelty in play materials so that mastering a toy with one objective might not meet all of the child's needs. Left to their own, children almost always prefer simple, open-ended play materials, as is proven every Christmas when the boxes become as fun as what is in them.

What should the play area look like?

The design of a play area has a tremendous effect on how the children act and behave. Large open areas encourage running and boisterous play. When uncontrolled running regularly occurs next to activities like block construction, trouble will follow. You can easily spot poor play area design when you visit programs, as there will be evidence of conflict and frustration among the children as they play. A checklist is provided in Appendix A to help you judge the appropriateness of play areas.

A play room should be large enough for children to work and play comfortably. The National Association for the Education of Young Children accreditation standards for centers recommends a minimum of thirty-five square feet per child, with a preferred space of fifty square feet. Family home childcare play rooms will vary greatly and it is up to you to decide if the space seems sufficient. There should be room enough for a child to play with the group, or to move off alone. Natural sunlight is desirable, as well as plants and aquariums to soften the environment. The room and its play materials should be arranged so that the child can understand how things are organized, with clearly marked storage areas that the children can get to without adult assistance.

Is television an appropriate activity?

Although many young children enjoy television, its use is not really suited to their learning style. Through television, the child receives information, but cannot experience it physically or directly. School age children and adults can learn in this visual manner (presuming there is something on television to learn), but preschool children need to hold, touch and feel in order for true learning to occur.

Parents often relate that their two- and three-year-old children have learned their numbers and letters from television, and this is true in one sense. A young child can learn letter recognition and even the corresponding sound by seeing and hearing them repeatedly. They can recite this material flawlessly, but the accomplishment is meaningless as children have no concept of what it is they have learned. If there is a benefit to this exercise, it is in the praise and attention that adults give for such performances, and the resulting boost in self-esteem.

For the most part, television is best used under your supervision at home. The visual stimulation does catch the young child's attention and provides time to tend to household chores or make dinner, but the time during the day at childcare is better spent in more appropriate ways.

An exciting exception to this is an excellent nationwide public television training program called the *Sesame Street*

Preschool Education Program. It is aired on public television channels in many cities and trains childcare providers to use television more effectively. They receive materials and training for activities to do with their children after the viewing of specific children's programs. In this way, the true learning style of the young child is used to extend the television viewing experience. More information on this program can be received by contacting the Preschool Education Program listed in Appendix B.

What is a reasonable standard of cleanliness?

The arrival of a new child in the family often means a revision of the previously held standard of cleanliness around the house. In fact, nothing seems to run quite the same once children arrive. A new balance has to be struck on the level of cleanliness that is acceptable to the family and each of its members.

In childcare, the problem intensifies with the number of bodies actively at play. A large part of the time is spent in activities like filling, dumping, building and tearing down play materials. This is how concepts like mass, volume and force are learned. The level of "mess" is also increased by the availability of more play choices than the average home would be likely to offer.

Be realistic in assessing play-related clutter, as opposed to real dirt, which is never acceptable under any circumstances. Weekly maintenance routines should include cleaning and disinfection of all tables, chairs and sleeping cots, mats or beds. The daily clean-up routine should include the re-sorting and returning all toys to their proper storage, and the clean-up of all floors, floor coverings and bathroom fixtures. In infants areas, all toys should be cleaned daily.

How much noise is too much noise?

The noise level is one of the first that you will notice when you visit childcare programs. Childcare noise is not like normal household noise. It includes the sounds of many children competing for play materials, attention and space. That is not to say that the noise is negative. Only when there is excessive yelling or crying should you be concerned, and the adults should always be modeling correct behavior in their verbal interactions with the children.

There are certain times of the day when crying and disagreements are more frequent among the children on a fairly regular basis. Right before lunch, when children are hungry and tired, is one such time. This is a good time to visit a program that you think you might be choosing, as you can observe how the adults are coping with the multiple demands of the group during a stressful period.

Laughter and excitement are signs of happy, healthy play and such noise, even when loud, is certainly welcomed by caregivers as a good sign, although you might find it somewhat unpleasant.

How are arrivals and departures monitored?

Many programs use sign-in and sign-out sheets to maintain a daily written record of attendance. In some states this procedure is required in the licensing guidelines. Large programs should have someone stationed near the main entrance to check who is coming in and out of the facility, particularly during the busiest arrival and departure hours. The faces of the regular parents become familiar to staff, and anyone else is quickly noticed.

How can I be sure that no one will pick up my child without my permission?

To back up arrival and departure procedures, files should be kept with the names of anyone who has permission to remove your child from the center. If someone different comes for your child, the file and an I.D. can be quickly and easily checked. If an emergency arises and you need to ask someone different to pick up your child, you can let the provider know by telephone, and the name and the I.D. can be checked at that time. Some newer centers have state-of-the-art security systems with electronic eyes or admittance by pass cards.

If your child is involved in any kind of a custody case, particularly if there is a restraining order, be sure to let your provider know. Show all pertinent papers to the provider and explain the situation in detail, including how you can be reached and under what circumstances you or the police should be called. Many providers have dealt with such issues before and will and understand the importance of protecting your child.

Are children ever taken from the childcare site during the day?

No child should be taken from a childcare site without your knowledge and prior consent. However, in the family home childcare setting it is fairly common for the provider to take children on daily outings and household errands. If your provider is going to do this, you might want to include it in your written contract agreement before you enroll your child. Many parents choose a home childcare setting for this very reason, as it provides the child with an array of common home experiences that are family related. If this is agreeable to you, be sure ask for evidence of insurance coverage, driving records and restraining devices in automobiles.

Because of liability concerns, most centers do not take children away from the center except for pre-arranged field trips and, for these, an advance permission slip should be required. A "blanket" permission slip is acceptable if there are going to be regularly scheduled excursions to neighborhood parks or libraries.

Do children have to participate in all the activities?

The desire to be involved in play varies widely from child to child, often depending on personality and previous play experience. It can take days, or even weeks, for a child to join into a new activity. Adults who work with young children should be accepting of these natural differences, and should never coerce participation. Efforts should be made to try to entice a child into activities, but the child should have the right to choose when they will join in. Sooner or later, the innate love of play wins out and the child is drawn into the flow. When the choice comes directly from the child, great gains are made in social maturity and self-esteem.

What are the most common behavior problems in childcare?

Young children are in the process of learning the kinds of behaviors that are considered appropriate by adults and society. This is a slow process which extends well into the teenage years, and even beyond. Children have to be taught what is expected of them, and these expectations might be different from those at home. The manner in which these lessons are taught largely determined the effectiveness of the lesson.

In the childcare setting, several recurring behavior issues appear on a consistent and ongoing basis as children adapt to the group, non-familial setting. Anticipating issues might help you to guide your child into the proper behaviors ahead of time. These include:

* Using appropriate language; refraining from name-calling, loud voices, screaming and interrupting
* Using the bathroom as intended, avoiding playing with water, toothpaste, soap and toilet tissue, which are a constant temptations
* Cleaning up messes after play
* Using materials carefully; not damaging and breaking things through careless use

How are discipline problems handled?

For young children, discipline should be used to teach appropriate behaviors, not to punish. This is one of the most sensitive issues in childcare, as adults often fall back on the discipline methods that were used by their own parents, whether or not these methods were appropriate. Many good opportunities to learn can be wasted when punishment takes the place of an explanation or correctly modeled behavior.

Children in childcare spend long periods of time in group play, and they do remarkably well coping and getting along. But sooner or later all children become short-tempered or angry when their immediate needs are not met. Social skills are still developing and even a normally cooperative child occasionally lashes out at a bothersome playmate or play situation. In other cases, because children cannot usually think in logical, reasoned ways, they do things "wrong" without ever being aware that they have done so.

Your child's behavior at home is not a guaranteed predictor of behavior at childcare, where there is far more activity and greater competition for attention. The caregivers in the program should have training to deal with the normal reactions of children to stress and group care. Children can never be allowed to hurt each other, or to destroy things that other children have created, but the reasons behind such actions need to be considered and understood before the situation is dealt with.

In most states it is illegal to physically discipline children in childcare, and caregivers have more appropriate alternatives than spanking, hitting and yelling. One commonly used technique in childcare is the removal of the child from the group, often called "time out". The child is actually physically removed, either to a separate part of the room or from the room, until becoming calm and choosing to return and begin to play again. If "time out" is used, the following parameters should accompany it:

1. Never use for children under two.
2. The exclusion should never be to a room where no adult is present.
3. The period of exclusion should be short; no more than one minute per year of age is a good rule of thumb.
4. The child should be able to choose when to return.
5. The child should be hugged and made to feel loved on returning.

Another alternative for inappropriate behavior is the use of alternative choices wherein the child is invited to seek solutions to their behavior problems. A number of studies into disciplining young children indicate that giving choices decreases aggressive behaviors. Asking questions like, "Where would it be safer to do this?" or "What else could we use this for?" allow the child to solve the issue at hand. Good discipline can often mean no more than talking things through and asking the child how to deal with the problem.

No discipline method should be used for children under age two, where other alternatives include redirecting, distracting, holding or rocking, and getting the child involved in another activity will generally work.

If a more serious behavior problem occurs, you should meet with the administrator and your child's caregiver to mutually agree on a plan of action, keeping in mind that behavior problems do not indicate a "bad" or "naughty" child. If the provider is indicating this, they do not have an appropriate background in child development.

No child is "bad." Misbehavior is a child's way of letting adults know that something in their life is wrong. It is up to the adults to provide the guidance and environment that will enable the child to deal with the situation.

If the problem that the child is dealing with is severe, it is possible that a regular childcare provider does not have the training to deal effectively with the behavior, in which case a child psychologist should be consulted.

Do children have to take a nap?

Programs for preschool children almost always have an afternoon period after lunch for resting or napping. The majority of children under age five sleep during that time. In some states offering a rest period is mandated by the licensing guidelines. While most adults would be thrilled with the prospect of a rest period after lunch, children do not usually see it that way. As with the evening bedtime at home, napping can cause resistance and unhappiness. Children who find napping especially distasteful might begin to resist an otherwise successful childcare experience.

Napping is necessary for most children, especially those who rise early so that their parents can commute to work. The typical childcare day is nine to twelve hours in length and even high energy children cannot cope with the group setting for that long without taking a break to recharge.

If you think that napping will cause resistance, discuss it with the caregiver rather than leaving your child to deal with it alone. Review your child's sleep patterns at home to see if any adjustment can be made to help your child work into the routines at childcare. Keeping your child up a little later might be less convenient to you, but might allow for your child to fit into the group schedule better. If your child really has given up napping, and some few children do so as early as age three, find out if quiet activities are offered for children who are not tired or cannot fall asleep. If a provider insists that all children sleep, this might be signal an inflexibility that carries over into other areas as well.

How is a child's cultural identity valued?

The link between a child's cultural identity and self esteem is well documented by research. This is part of the reason why you probably wish your child could be at home with you or another family member. The home is the place that intimately reflects the beliefs and values that you wish your child to acquire. Unless childcare can offer some of the same familiarity to the child, the adjustment can be more difficult.

Many resources are available to caregivers to help them understand and prepare for the variety of cultures that need childcare in America today. Publications, workshops and formal college courses address multicultural sensitivity.

Ask potential providers how they can meet your child's individual needs for cultural awareness and recognition. Multicultural sensitivity is an element that is carefully examined in both the home and center accreditation processes. A quality program will have play equipment that reflects the cultural diversity of all children who come there. Books, dolls, toys and food menus served should seem familiar to every child in the group.

Should children have a caregiver who speaks their own language?

Young children, especially those under age two, are extremely well adapted to the task of learning language. At no other time in life will the language learning ability function so effectively. Preschool children have been known to acquire two and three languages simultaneously with relative ease, and without confusing or running them together.

A caregiver who does not speak your family's primary language, but who is good in other important ways, should be considered primarily on those merits. As long as you are providing good language models within your family in your own primary language, the child will not be negatively affected.

Do children in childcare get sick more often?

There is no way to keep children from catching an occasional cold, and because childcare programs are designed for children who are in good health, there will be days when the service will not be able to meet your needs. Programs for mildly ill children have been struggling to survive since the mid 1980s, predominantly sponsored by major employers or hospitals. Because they are costly to operate and costly to use, their success has been minimal.

All children become ill from time to time because they are grouped indoors with other children, increasing their exposure to germs. Precautions can be taken to minimize germs, but group care for young children cannot, and should not, be expected to be an aseptic atmosphere.

Evidence suggests that after about two years, children in childcare develop some immunity to respiratory illnesses, and children four and five years old with several years of childcare behind them are sturdy and living proof of this. However, children under three, especially those with siblings, do seem to wind up with a higher than average incidence of illness.

What precautions are taken to minimize illness?

Over time, children will acquire a certain amount of immunity from playing in groups. Many become surprisingly disease-resistant, but not all fare so well. Repeated exposure to illness can be hard on some children. In some cases it is advisable to switch to a care situation with fewer children until the child gets older.

The spread of infectious disease can be curtailed through good health and hygiene practices, and you should see evidence of such policies when you visit programs. Look for such things as:

* teaching children to cover their nose and mouth when sneezing
* availability of tissues for runny noses
* sanitary maintenance and cleaning procedures
* proper heating and cooling systems
* proper food preparation and storage
* sterilization of dishes
* handwashing for adults and children, especially with meals and toileting
* use of liquid, rather than solid soap
* frequent handwashing when a child has a cold

Remember to keep your own child at home when signs of illness appear. It is difficult for a young child who is coming down with an illness to cope with the noise and activity of childcare. A sound diet and plenty of rest can also go a long way toward keeping your child healthy.

Are head lice infestations common?

Head lice make an occasional appearance from time to time in many childcare programs, even in those with the highest cleanliness standards. Head lice do not reflect dirty children or poor hygiene. They are often introduced by a child who has played with an infected friend in the home neighborhood. Because young children wrestle and hug, the infected child quickly passes the lice to others.

If your child does get head lice, the symptoms will include constant itching and small white eggs at the base of the hairline and neck areas. Over-the-counter lice treatment shampoos work well, or you can ask your pediatrician to recommend a specific product.

Parents are usually notified immediately of the problem and are expected to pick up their child for treatment. Most will allow the child to return as soon as the shampoo treatment is administered and all eggs have been removed from the hair.

The other, more bothersome part of the treatment includes treating all bedclothes, hats, pillows and stuffed animals at home and at childcare. If this is not done, re-infestation (and another phone call at work) can occur. Pillows, hats and such can be treated by tossing them in a hot clothes dryer for forty-five minutes, or by sealing them tightly in a plastic bag for several weeks.

Bedclothes, including blankets and bedspreads need to be washed in hot, soapy water.

How is HIV/AIDS addressed?

The subject of the AIDS virus in childcare is addressed by professional organizations in the child development field at conferences and in college course work. At this time, the Pediatric AIDS Foundation says that transmission of the HIV virus in the childcare setting is not an area of major concern by those who study and track the disease.

They stress that AIDS is not passed among young children through kissing, sneezing, drinking fountains, toilet seats, or by sharing food.

If young children ask about AIDS, they probably are not interested in abstract ideas or facts about adult sexual behaviors. It is usually not necessary to explain the disease in detail. What children need to know is that they are not at risk and should be relieved of all groundless AIDS-related anxiety.

What about Sudden Infant Death Syndrome (SIDS)?

The cause of SIDS remains a mystery although it strikes and estimated 7,000 to 8,000 apparently healthy babies each year in the United States. SIDS rarely strikes under one month and it peaks at age two to three months. It diminishes at about six months and is almost entirely gone by one year. It is slightly more common in preemie babies, boys and children living in poverty. Smoking during pregnancy is now largely suspect, according to a Pennsylvania State medical study.

Do children in childcare get hurt more often?

The childcare setting provides more exposure to the kinds of activities where injuries happen. Few homes have the challenging climbing equipment or high slides found at many programs. Also, children in groups play rougher and take greater risks.

One of the major tasks of early childhood is to develop and master physical skills like running and climbing. In fact, the calcium consumed in the diet cannot by utilized by the child's bones without the presence of sufficient vigorous, regular exercise. To encourage these skills and proper bone formation, vigorous outdoor play is necessary and encouraged. It is inevitable that some children will get bumped and scraped in the process.

Some children are actually "accident prone", a condition that occurs in roughly three in 10,000 children, according to a University of San Francisco study of 55,000 children. Accidents also tend to happen in clusters and during times of life transitions, of which childcare would certainly qualify.

What measures can enhance children's safety?

Rules for safety need to be part of the children's predictable daily routine. They need to know what the limits are, what the safety rules are, and why they are enforced. Safety should be a regular part of the curriculum where the group sits down together and discusses safety concerns as they occur and in preparation for field trips and outdoor play. Young children cannot always anticipate what is safe and what is not, and it takes repeated reminding to enforce even the simplest concepts.

Safety is also more than educating the children. An adult level of responsibility should be present in supervision, especially during outdoor play. Adults who stand around and chat with co-workers can miss seeing dangerous situations developing. Adult behavior during outside play time is a good indication of the safety level of the program.

Because many accidents happen in the outdoor play areas where the most vigorous play takes place, it is wise to do a careful maintenance check of these areas. Your child will be spending a great deal of the day in these areas and if hazards exist, they can usually be detected ahead of time. A checklist of things to examine on playgrounds is found in Appendix A.

What is the most common cause of accidental death among children under the age of five?

Parents are usually surprised to hear that SIDS or poisoning are not the major causes of early accidental death. Choking on food is actually the primary danger, which emphasizes the necessity for the childcare provider to be certified in first aid.

Hot dogs are the greatest offender, followed by hard candy, peanuts, popcorn and peanut butter, which can ball up and get stuck in the airway. A child should have molar teeth before eating these foods.

If a child gets hurt, how does the parent find out what happened?

Your childcare provider should have a clear and consistent system for informing you about any accidents that happen to your child. Information about the circumstances of the incident should be noted in writing at the time of the accident by the adult in charge. If an adult did not witness the accident, that should also be noted. In spite of the best of efforts, the adults in even high quality programs do not always see everything that goes on. However, it is probably cause for concern if repeated accidents occur and they are never seen by an adult.

If a visible mark like a lump or bruise results, you should be called at work so you are not unpleasantly surprised at the end of the day. A sample accident form can be found in Appendix A. If your provider does not have a form you might ask that it be used for your child.

Can children bring their favorite belongings?

Children love to bring personal items to childcare. In fact, many children will not leave home in the morning unless they have something personal and special in their pockets or hands. Unfortunately, children do come with items that their parents obviously do not know about, like sets of keys, fine jewelry and credit cards. The excitement of "show-and-tell" just gets to children sometimes.

Help your child pick out items that are appropriate to take the night before, and do a quick pocket check each morning. Some appropriate items include storybooks, small stuffed animals, and inexpensive little toys.

Always check with your caregiver before you send anything, as there might be rules about what and when personal items can be brought. Some caregivers have a particular day each week to share personal items.

Some younger children are particularly attached to a blanket, teddy bear, or other comfort item from home. Such items provide solace and reassurance in the face of stresses like separation and bedtime. The item is something that the child owns. It is usually something soft and portable and can become worn and ragged, a source of embarrassment to the parent.

Many children have such items between twelve and eighteen months, although some children never express an interest in them at all. Girls and boys attach to them equally and the items are usually self-selected, rather than given by the parent.

These items should be accepted into childcare for the younger children and will be discarded by the child when he or she is ready. Most children give them up completely or at least use them only at home by age five, when social activities begin to predominate.

How do children keep track of their belongings?

In childcare, the burden for keeping track of belongings is on the child, and to most parents' surprise, this works quite well. To assist your child in learning self-responsibility, you can follow a few simple guidelines:

1. Check to see what your child is carrying out the door each morning.
2. Send only non-valuable, replaceable items.
3. Buy a good, black permanent marker and label everything that goes to childcare, including underwear. Consider how hard it is to identify the owners of twelve navy blue hooded sweatshirts!
4. Help your child put personal belongings into his or her cubbie (storage) area each morning.
5. Help your child retrieve all items from the cubbie at the end of the day.
6. Tell your child how proud you are for his or her good habits.

How can parents get specific information about the day?

Caregivers normally have regular ways of transmitting information to the parents of their children. Unfortunately, some parents are too busy to access them. Methods include such faithful regulars as bulletin boards, newsletters, folders and daily written summaries. Any of these which are regularly used should be explained as part of the initial interview.

But when this information falls short of the more personal stories and anecdotes that you would like to hear about your child's day, some targeted questions can help you get the information that you want, or can shed light on specific concerns. For instance:

"Jamie is usually playing with Bobby when I pick her up. Are they best friends? Who else does she play with?"

"Did Mary have a favorite activity today?"

"Did Johnny play with blocks today?"
"How is Sarah handling her anger?"

Who decides when a child is ready for toilet training?

This question is really quite simple, because toilet training will not work unless it is a mutual decision of all parties involved. You should never feel pressured to begin to toilet train your child before you think you are both ready. Everyone can watch for signs of readiness until all agree that it is time to begin. Common readiness signs include:

* asking to have wet or soiled clothing removed
* staying dry for longer periods
* waking up dry from naps
* having fairly regular bowel movements
* pulling down own clothing
* showing an awareness that bowel movement or urination is occurring

Readiness varies anywhere from toddler-hood up to four years of age, with most children training somewhere between two and three years of age. The child's nervous system is rarely ready before at least eighteen months. Talking ability is also necessary so that the child can connect the spoken word with the internal feeling.

Toilet training requires patience because results are sporadic and accidents happen for the whole first year after the seeming success. Toilet training should never be a part of a curriculum or group exercise. When the signs are clear and the child is ready, the process is easy. If not, there can be an unimaginable struggle of wills, and the child always wins! Because there is no absolute timetable for readiness, no single group of two-year-old children would ever be likely to be ready to try at the same time.

When you both agree to start, your first step will be to discuss and agree on the same "rules", and devise a means of daily written communication. Dress your child in loose clothing and send plenty of training pants, all clearly marked with your child's name. Remember that this is a 100 percent commitment on both sides, and no diapers should be allowed except for at nap times.

You can help your provider by taking care of a few things on your end of the process like buying cotton underwear, teaching your child to raise and lower pants and underwear, and carrying a lightweight portable potty, toilet paper and can of disinfectant spray in your trunk.

If you use a family home childcare, you can probably purchase a potty chair just like the one at home for use during the day. In a center, this is not usually acceptable for sanitary reasons, but toilets there are small and child-sized. As you work together with the caregiver, use the same words to talk about toileting to the child and handle accidents in the same, nonchalant, non-punitive manner.

What happens if a child has a toileting accident?

While a child is in the process of toilet training, and for some time afterwards, accidents should be expected. However, toileting accidents are not just the private realm of two-year-old children. It is a rare preschooler who does not also have an occasional accident while engrossed in play. For the four or five year old, this is extremely embarrassing as they do not want to be called a baby.

Regardless of the child's age, such accidents should be handled quietly and without fuss. Depending on the age of the child, a certain amount of responsibility can be given for dealing with the accident by allowing them to remove their own wet clothes, put them in a plastic bags, or put on dry clothes stored in the personal cubbie. A two year old can get dry clothes, but should not be made to struggle at pulling wet clothes over wet shoes. The idea is not to punish, but rather to teach responsibility and a sense of self worth. Handwashing should always be a part of toileting routines, strictly monitored and modeled by the caregiver.

What happens to the child who refuses to toilet train?

Few caregivers are prepared for the eventuality of a three or four year old who has frequent accidents, but some children simply do not want to take the time to learn self-toileting. It is not necessarily a matter of being unwilling to cooperate, although this can happen as a result of starting too young or making the training a struggle of wills. Sometimes children get too engaged in what they are doing to feel the physical signs that should send them scurrying for the bathroom.

The self-esteem of these children is at risk for a situation that they really might not even be able to correct. If the childcare is at a center, keeping them back with younger children is not only cruel, but also developmentally inappropriate as it deprives them of peer stimulation and proper play materials.

Teasing, belittling and coaxing in front of the other children can damage self-esteem and make children angry. A late trainer should be checked by the pediatrician to be certain there is no physical cause for the delayed toileting control. If there are no physical problems, the child should be calmly and matter-of-factly given the responsibility for changing clothes when an accident occurs. Plenty of clean, dry clothing should be accessible to the child, along with plastic bags for wet or soiled clothing. Only in extreme cases of soiling should the adult intervene in the process. By taking full responsibility in a non-threatening atmosphere, the child will eventually solve the issue independently. This situation is both stressful and embarrassing for the parent, but as a pediatrician once told me, "No child goes off to college before being toilet trained." If it is any consolation, he is right.

How can parents deal with jealous feelings toward the caregiver?

Most parents cannot help but feel a little jealous when their child runs willingly into the arms of the caregiver. Parents choose a caregiver based on the belief that the person will do a great job. Parents want childcare to be as much like the care they give at home as possible. Unfortunately, when childcare succeeds in doing just that, ambivalent feelings can arise. Jealous reactions directed to caregivers are so common, they are the subject of a much current research.

Most parents can sit down and do a pretty good job of rationalizing themselves out of these feelings. Problems of a serious nature only arise if the parent begins to respond by exhibiting behaviors that are detrimental to the child's care situation, as a result of these feelings. Such behavioral changes can be on a subconscious level. They exhibit themselves in attempts to set the caregiver up for failure.

Some of the more common ways of undermining the

caregiver include keeping an infant up late or underfeeding, so that the child arrives in an irritable state. By sending a child in a soiled diaper that results in a diaper rash, the parent is justified in feeling resentful. Another technique is giving instructions that are so minute that no one could possibly follow them, implicitly suggesting that the caretaker cannot do as good a job as the parent.

New parents do not always feel confident about their parenting skills. Unlike the caregiver, who balances multiple children with seeming ease, new parents usually have to make mistakes and learn as they go. Their tenuous confidence is easily undermined in the face of caregiver criticism, which intensifies their guilt.

It is important to deal with jealous feeling openly so they do not undermine the care situation and the parent/provider partnership. Through regular, sensitive communication and mutual support of each other in your individual roles, you can learn to share the joy that is your child, relishing successes and accomplishments with your provider. A child's love is not earned through meticulous, knowledgeable methodologies, but rather by warm and loving interludes. Any new parent is equipped to do this, and no caregiver can improve on the benefits of this natural bond.

How do caregivers deal with negative feelings toward parents?

Sometimes after the caregiver has worked hard all day to make the child feel loved and comfortable, the parent comes in a bad mood, or reacts out of left-over job stress or heavy traffic. Being underpaid and unvalued, it is easy to understand how child caregivers might sometimes feel that their parents do not know and love the children as much as they do.

The odd part is that while these dynamics are going on, both partners in the child's care are probably doing an excellent job and the child is probably developing well thanks to the good efforts of both. Only through communication and trust, both of which take time, can the parents and caregivers come to see the beauty in their relationship of sharing in a child's wondrous growth.

SPECIAL CONSIDERATIONS

Most of the material in this book relates most directly to the preschool child between the ages of two and five. For children who are either younger or older than this, there are some very important considerations in matching the care to their developmental stage.

Infant and Toddler Care

What is meant by "infant?"

An infant, in the childcare system, generally refers to a child under age two years. Infancy is further broken down into two stages, pre-crawling and moving (toddler).

Why does infant care deserve special attention?

The care of infants by persons other than the parents or immediate family is a fairly recent phenomenon. For the first time in our history, over half of all children under age two now have mothers in the workforce. The demand for infant care has risen steadily along with the working-mother trend. What this means for the children and families growing up in these new ways is uncertain. Research into the effects of non-parental childcare for infants and toddlers is in its early stages, and the results are mixed at this time. In the very least, it is known that programs for infants and toddlers show a wider range in quality than services to older preschool children.

Quality infant and toddler care is not scaled down preschool care. Infancy encompasses a time of rapid physical and mental development when the freedom to explore the environment is essential. Infants need highly individualized, personal care. They have urgent physical, emotional and developmental needs which cannot wait. Caregivers must be stable and their turnover needs to be minimized.

Parents should know exactly what to look for because the choice of infant care is critical to the child's sense of basic trust. Unfortunately, this important decision must be made in a market where there is a shortage of infant care, and especially of quality infant care.

Two major themes emerge from an examination of published materials for infant caregiver training. First, care should focus on the developmental milestones of infancy. Second, the infant should have help in developing into a social being who can manage feelings and express individuality. Both areas help to develop positive self-concepts and feelings of worth.

Some studies warn that a weak bond can develop between the parent and child if they are separated for long periods of time. Other research points toward greater success and autonomy in later school endeavors for children who have been in high quality infant/toddler programs. For many parents, such conflicting research increases feelings of guilt at a time when they may not have the choice to stay at home. Regardless of who is right, if your child must be in childcare, finding the highest quality care is the most productive way to deal with any unknown risk.

Are some childcare settings more suitable for infants and toddlers than others?

Care by a relative is usually the first choice of parents of infants, although the lack of nearby relatives often eliminates this choice. Care by an unrelated person in the home is often the next choice, but cost can make that unrealistic, as well.

With home childcare and centers remaining, most child development experts would lean towards the home childcare setting as the more appropriate choice in most cases for infants and toddlers. In a home childcare setting the group size is often smaller, the family style setting is retained, and sleeping and eating arrangements more closely resemble those of the child's home. The home childcare setting allows for a better chance for personal care and mental stimulation. It also seems that the flexibility needed for children under age two is easier to achieve in a noninstitutional setting.

Any infant care choices can work well if special attention is paid to the group size. Being in too large a group can overstimulate an infant, causing a lot of crying and creating a difficult care situation. Infants and toddlers need a calm, human environment with leisurely, suitable routines. Such an atmosphere can be difficult to achieve in a larger group or institutional settings.

What is bonding?

Bonding is a term used by researchers to describe the attachment that develops between the infant and its caregivers. In a nutshell, bonding is the way in which babies fall in love. It is largely a physical phenomenon grounded in such behaviors as eye contact and physical handling. Bonding gives the infant a sense of security which allows for trust and exploration of the larger world.

Parents who expect bonding to follow naturally and quickly right after birth might be relieved to hear there is no single, magical moment in which bonding occurs, but rather a connection formed over the course of many ordinary days. Three of the most common tasks of caring for the new child — feeding, touching, and playing — are intimately connected with the bonding process.

How does bonding relate to nonparental care?

Because feeding, touching and playing trigger bonding attachments, persons other than the parents can also experience bonding. For example, who could question a grandparent or sibling's bond to an infant? Such bonds are termed "secondary," and they enhance the primary bonds but never displace them.

It appears that the infant will bond with all who respond to their basic needs. It is important to understand that the bond established with the parent is never weakened or lessened by other secondary bonds, or by hours spent away from them. Infants appear to have a enormous capacity to love.

A recent study from the University of Minnesota Institute of Child Development adds to a growing body of evidence showing that a warm, responsive caregiver allows the baby to separate from the parent without harm. The proper caregiver can even lessen the stress experienced by the infant at separation from the parents. Caregiver sensitivity is emerging as a key factor in defining high quality infant care.

Is it possible to find care for a six-week-old infant?

Returning to work six weeks after childbirth is not desirable for either the mother or the child. If you have to return to work this early, and you cannot find a relative to care for your infant, home childcare programs do take infants this young. Special attention should be given to provider stability, so that early changes of caregivers can be avoided.

What is the most important consideration in choosing an infant/toddler program?

Without question, the caregiver is the most important ingredient in quality infant and toddler care. The child will change as a result of interactions with the caregiver, and you want those changes to be positive.

As you visit programs, you will see a variety of educational materials that promise to stimulate and enhance infant development. You will be urged to consider the benefits of particular infant development philosophies. The simple truth is that infants are "programmed" to develop optimally if their basic physical and emotional needs are met. It is not necessary to worry about educating infants with specially designed materials or programs.

What your infant does need is a caregiver who delights in the individual person who your baby is. Your child's main developmental task will be to gain a sense of trust in people and in the world in general. Success in this task will go a long way in assuring success in later development. If caregivers feel caught up in a routine cycle of endless feedings, diaper changes and chores, they cannot still the infant's anguish of an empty stomach or other frightened feelings.

Do not be dazzled by bright colors and marketing gimmicks. Focus your attention on finding the right person to care for your child. Look for a proven track record of staying on the job, combined with knowledge and training. This is the bottom line in finding the quality care your infant or toddler needs and deserves.

Since babies cannot talk, how do parents know what goes on all day?

Spoken language does not appear for some time, but infants and toddlers are already keen communicators. Researchers have noted a recognizable difference in the frightened birth cry and the annoyed or angry cry a few minutes later as the baby is cleaned. Communication begins at birth and is modified and expanded as the child grows and develops.

Infants are attentive listeners and superb interpreters of body language. Without speaking, the child can give you enough feedback to determine its message and the need at any particular time. It is not hard to read the signs of a happy baby, or of one who is hungry, frightened or tense. You can also learn a great deal about what babies will be doing by looking at the materials available during the day. There should be a choice of toys which encourage looking, listening, sucking, mouthing and touching. Play spaces should be large and open with as few barriers to exploration as practical.

Evaluating how your young child's day goes can also be accomplished by watching how your child and the other children react to the caregiver. Evidence of affection like snuggling, laughing and direct eye contact should be present. Formal, regular communication should be exchanged daily. Caregivers can jot down little anecdotes about what happens during the day, in addition to routine information about feeding, napping and diapering routines. If you can receive short phone calls at work during the day, so much the better.

Above all, never allow the daily interactions with the caregiver to become superficial and meaningless. So much is happening at this time in your child's life! As you come to trust the caregiver, it is tempting to shift more responsibility in that direction and to lessen your role in making the childcare work. Your child learns new things every single day, and you can be a part of that learning by exchanging information with the caregiver in a warm and meaningful way.

Are infants ever disciplined?

Never should any type of discipline be used in an infant program. For the first six months, distracting should work in most instances. By eight or nine months, limits can begin to be defined in a gentle way through speech and removal of the object or child from the object at issue.

You should discuss the rules you use at home with your caregiver so that you can both be consistent. For example, if the baby is not allowed to touch the television at home, the same rule should apply at childcare. It is also important to remember that a child under one year might understand a command like "no," but that does not mean that this can be translated into a corresponding action. In other words, the baby might hear and understand a request not to touch something, but might still need to be physically moved or need to have the object taken away.

How is time spent in an infant program?

Infants need to eat when they are hungry, to be comforted when they are frightened, hurt or upset, and to sleep when they are tired. Within this framework, the individual pace of each child should be respected and accommodated. Organized group activities at this age are inappropriate. Babies like to spend time exploring themselves and each other, and making social overtures, like touching, mouthing, making eye contact, taking and giving toys.

While awake, infants enjoy being talked to and held. Appropriate toys should be available, and rotated so that different items appear each day. Time should be spent rocking in the arms of the caregiver, listening to music, and experiencing calm, pleasant touches. A window out into the real world is fun for infants who are scooting across the floor and beginning to pull themselves up.

Scooting, crawling and walking should always be encouraged through the careful placement of safe, sturdy props. The use of playpens is not conducive to exploratory activities. Walkers, which have been proven to be extremely unsafe, should never be used.

Inborn sleep patterns vary widely. Every baby differs

in the amount of sleep needed and there is no such thing as too little sleep if the child is healthy and is being allowed to follow natural sleep rhythms. Newborns sleep anywhere from ten to seventeen hours a day with the amount decreasing with age. During the first two to three months, naps last as long as three and four hours.

What kinds of toys stimulate infant development?

The best toy for any infant is the caregiver, and the youngest of babies requires nothing else. For young babies, the sights, sounds and movements of the environment are stimulating enough. They especially enjoy looking at the facial features of the caregiver. When toys are appropriate they can include simple additions like bright scarves hung above the crib, soft balls, squeeze toys, plastic spoons and keys, and soft plastic rings.

Older babies need few toys as well. They are intrigued by their own hands, feet and bodies. Crawlers and cruisers like to scoot over pillows and mattresses and also need rails and sturdy furniture to pull up on. Toys are used for looking, mouthing, grasping and touching, not for any inherent play value. Objects two to five inches in size, and containers to put them in, are especially enjoyable and appropriate. Other suggestions include shower curtain rings, plastic blocks, small dolls, balls of various sizes, nesting blocks, pots and pans, discarded boxes, large Leggos and beginners books.

How much room do babies need?

Before babies start to scoot and crawl, space is not much of a problem. But when they start moving, things at home and at childcare change for forever. Babies begin to move at their own pace and in their own, sometimes comical, ways. From a biological point of view, muscular readiness and temperament play a role. From an environmental aspect, encouragement and materials can tempt a baby to get moving.

The main consideration with space is that the emerging abilities to move have ample space for expression. For scooting, crawling and walking, babies need a safe, clean section of flooring.

Can babies be spoiled by being handled too much?

Babies cannot be spoiled by being handled; they can only be taught that the world is a caring and responsive place and that their needs will be met by the adults in it. Touch is a primary component of healthy infant development. Because infant group care demands that the needs of several babies be met, it is important that the caregiver you choose is fully and personally committed to touching as a primary goal.

Ask infant caregivers about their beliefs and views on infant care. Also, be sure to watch how they handle the children by making several unannounced visits before you make your selection.

Are there any special health considerations for infants in childcare?

Babies do not respond to colds and viral infections in the same way as older children. Sick babies cannot tell anyone that they do not feel well and symptoms need to be identified by the adult in charge. Not all babies run a fever when they are sick, and anything over 100 degrees merits a call to the parent.

Other symptoms of illness include crankiness, loss of appetite, crying and tugging at the ears, listlessness, and long periods of sleep. As the parent, you are probably already aware of the special ways in which your child exhibits the onset of illness, and you should share that information with the caregiver.

Ear infections are one of the most common complications of colds in infants. The passages between the ears and nose are easily blocked by mucus. Even after treatment by antibiotics, excess fluid can remain in the ear, affecting the baby's hearing and response to sounds.

Can mothers continue to breastfeed?

Mothers should never be discouraged by their provider to discontinue breastfeeding for the caregiver's convenience. But in the interest of the child's adjustment, weaning in preparation for any bottle feedings that will have to take place at childcare should be undertaken early enough so that they are as stress-free as possible. By allowing the milk to taper off gradually, the baby can have plenty of time to learn this new way of feeding.

If one feeding is dropped every week before the child begins childcare, the desired level can be comfortably reached. If the child does not cooperate, nipples of different shapes can be tried and the father or other family member can try to take over those feedings. With bottle feedings, there should continue to be an abundance of cuddling and the bottle should never be propped.

At about five to six months, sips from a cup can be begun and an empty plastic cup can join the stock of toys.

Who should introduce new foods?

New foods should be introduced at home, one at a time in any given week, so that any allergic reactions will be easily noted. When you are certain that the new food is being tolerated, it can be given at childcare was well. Whole milk usually replaces formula at the end of the first year. At this point, most caregivers will provide the milk.

How can a safe crib be identified?

More infants die each year in accidents involving cribs than in any other nursery product. Cribs can be checked when you visit programs by using the Crib Safety Checklist found in Chapter 6. Be sure to take a measuring tape with you when you visit, as you will need to check several critical measurement features on the crib structure.

What needs to be brought from home each day?

Individual providers will have their own set of expectations as to who is responsible for providing certain essential items each day. Diaper and food policies need to be carefully discussed and outlined in the contract. Beyond the basics you might be expected to bring some or all of the following:

* extra sets of clothing, marked with your child's name
* extra empty bottles
* comb or brush
* topical solutions for diapering
* pacifiers
* teething rings/toys
* bibs
* small blanket

How do toddlers spend their time in childcare?

The most common reason for moving a child from an infant room to a toddler room in a childcare center is that it is difficult to mix movers and non-movers in a group setting. If these two stages of infancy are combined, safety policies need to be in place to protect the less mobile children. Toddlers are enthusiastic and curious with their newfound ability to move, and are particularly interested in touching the facial features of other children. Toddlers need constant adult attention, encouragement and love. They are not yet ready for group activities which last more than a few minutes. They might play next to another child, but true interaction is minimal and sharing is impossible. They can usually eat together at one time, and nap together after the noontime meal, if flexibility is allowed for the occasional individual variations.

Playtime should be filled with cheerful noises and bustling activity, of which a favorite is dumping and filling. It is also appropriate and common for toddlers to simply watch or stare at the activities of other children. The mouth remains a major tool for exploring new objects, and fingers can get into the tiniest cracks. As parents will attest, a single straight pin on a rug can be located by any toddler.

Too many toys and too much stimulation can cause irritability, and a loving and welcoming lap needs to be available on a moments notice. Finally, toilet training will begin for a few children, but should not be a part of any toddler program curriculum.

What sort of toys do toddlers need?

Toddlers like lots of hand-sized objects in containers so that they can fill, transport, and dump them. This is a play activity of which toddlers never tire, and through which they gain a sense of predictability about size and weight. Materials need to be down on their level and readily accessible without adult assistance. Some suggested materials for their use include jumbo pegs and pegboards, plastic animal farms, jumbo Leggos, jumbo beads, small cars and trucks, one- to five-piece puzzles, snap beads, large plastic nuts and bolts, dolls, and balls of all sizes.

What is a good group size for infants and toddlers?

Group size is not the same as the ratio of adults to children. While three or four infants per adult can be an acceptable ratio, a group size of twenty infants in one room would not be acceptable because of the noise and activity levels. Twelve is probably a maximum size for a workable infant program. Toddlers and twos can probably handle a slightly larger number if it is a quality program. Infants, toddlers, and even two-year-old children have limited coping abilities. Too much noise and activity can become overwhelming and frightening. Furthermore, any crying that starts in an infant and toddler group is prone to spread quickly, adding to the confusion.

A slightly larger toddler program can work satisfactorily if children are physically spread out to play in smaller groups, and if the individual child can cope with the added noise.

How are biters and aggressive children handled?

Biting is a common problem in infant and toddler care. It appears with varying frequency and is upsetting to the children, the parents and caregivers. While some of the biting can be attributed to teething, it is also not uncommon for toddlers to resort to biting in times of stress or frustration. A child who comes to childcare without previous play experience, (which includes most toddlers), can react to the difficulty in learning to cope with the group experience in this way.

The child's play experience, or lack thereof, is information that should be shared with the caregiver before the child arrives. Sometimes a little more attention and holding is an effective way to combat biting. But if biting persists, strategic planning with the parents and staff needs to be done quickly. The purpose of these meetings is not to punishing the offending child. Rather, it is a means of helping the unhappy child find another way of acting out, or of identifying and removing the cause of the stress. Occasionally, the only solution is to change care situations. An actively biting toddler, placed in a smaller care situation for a few months, can often integrate back into the larger group successfully at a later date.

Bites can pose a health consideration, and all bite wounds should be cleansed thoroughly with soap. A doctor should be consulted if the skin is broken.

Can children bring security objects like blankets?

Many children cope with stress or change by attaching to security objects, like blankets. The object becomes a source of comfort when the child is alone, particularly at bedtime. The child usually wants to take the security object everywhere, and substitute items are vigorously resisted. Caregivers are accustomed to seeing security objects, and rarely object, as they make the transition from home to childcare easier.

An increased dependency on the security item can usually be dealt with by giving extra affection. This is not the time to make your child give up a cherished item. As children grow into preschool age, the dependency decreases naturally. Insisting on the object at age four or five causes some danger of teasing by peers, and use should be limited to home or bedtime at this point.

Can toddlers use a bottle as a security object?

For infants, bottles are an obvious necessity, serving both emotional and nutritional needs. For toddlers, anything other than a naptime bottle poses a sanitary problem. Toddlers are strong enough to grab bottles from other children, and smart enough to run away once they get them.

Can they bring pacifiers?

Infants have a need for sucking that is unrelated to food and nourishment. They enjoy the activity and soothes and helps them to quiet themselves. However, children who are used to a pacifier face genuine health concerns if they bring them to childcare. While the provider might tolerate their use, the potential of a shared pacifier remains high. It is virtually impossible to assure that the pacifier will end up in only your child's mouth, or that your child will not grab another child's. Unless this is the only way that a child can be consoled, it is best to leave it at home.

Are all toddlers fussy eaters?

Toddlers often announce their independence by taking firm stands on what they will or will not eat. They may show some strange food preferences and seem to prefer frequent, but small amounts of food. A childcare provider needs to take this into account when mixing them with older children who manage well on regularly scheduled meals at which they eat sometimes surprisingly enormous amounts.

Finger foods have the strongest appeal as they cater to the mode of independence. Food should never be a cause for struggle and toddlers should never be forced to eat. In fact, it is doubtful that they could be forced! Familiar foods are dearly loved and it is fine to serve the same thing over and over if it is nutritious. Foods cut into shapes and brightly colored food also hold special appeal. New foods are best presented at the beginning of the meal when the child is most hungry.

How do infants and toddlers react to beginning a new childcare program?

Before eight or nine months, babies usually offer a mild protest, if any, at being left with another caregiver. After that age, you can count on a loud complaint from your child. On a positive note, in nearly every case even the hardest criers settle down within a few minutes of the parent's departure. It is never easy to leave an infant, but if the transition to childcare is planned, the struggle and guilt can be kept to a minimum.

How can separation problems be minimized?

Anything that brings the idea of home to childcare will help the child to cope with the newness of the situation. Part of this process will include some detailed talks with your provider before you start. If the provider cannot arrange time for this, you might consider moving on and finding someone who can.

Knowing your baby's favorite songs or games, like peek-a-boo, can be a great help in the first few critical days. Knowing if the child is used to sleeping in a darkened room, or if crying is a part of the pre-sleep pattern, can also help to make your baby more comfortable. Your tips on how you diaper and how much is generally eaten at a time are critical to the transition. You might even want to write these things down so that the caregiver can refer back to them when necessary.

Make fifteen minute to thirty minute visits with your child during the two weeks before actually starting childcare and sit on the floor with the children so that your child sees that you are comfortable there. Separation can also be eased by following the same simple and quiet approach every day once you do start full time. Your separation routine should take no more than about ten minutes and might go something like this:

1. Greet the caregiver. If your child turns away, don't force eye contact. Chat casually, showing the child that you trust this person.
2. Settle in with your child. Put away personal belongings and remove jackets and hats.
3. Tell your child that you need to leave and that you will return. This isn't as silly as it sounds, because young children need verbal assurance as well as hugs. Pass your child to the caregiver, and leave. Respect your child's ability to cope. Call later if you need further assurance.

What if separation gets more difficult?

Occasionally, children have a more difficult time adjusting than their parents are prepared for. The separation process can take anywhere from a few days to several months, and one successful separation does not mean your troubles are over. Infants and toddlers experience setbacks when they are tired or not feeling well, and a busy weekend can have a visibly negative effect. If it is any consolation, separation problems peak between nine and twenty-four months, so better times lie ahead.

Helpless, guilty feelings that you experience should not be denied. Tell your child, even your infant, that you know that it makes him or her sad when you leave. By accepting your feelings, you can better accept your child's ambivalence and confusion. Successful bonding makes time apart difficult, but in time it becomes clear that this bond cannot be broken. Conflicting feelings are normal, but you are not giving up your child. You are only sharing.

If your child seems to be taking longer than usual to adjust, talk to the caregiver frequently. If everyone really tries, and it still does not work, the situation might need to be re-examined and a more appropriate setting found to respond to the child's special needs.

School Age Programs

What is school age childcare like?

Ten years ago only a few elementary schools saw a link between what children did during the school day and how they spent their time away from school. Now every school district in the country is grappling with integrating the needs of the child's whole day into their educational planning. Many of the educational problems of the classroom are conclusively linked to the hours spent outside of school. Providing before and after school programs is one effective response being explored by many of these districts.

Centers for school age children are often found at or near elementary school sites. Many family home childcare services are also located near the school to cater to the school age child's need for services. Because of the more advanced developmental level of these children, there is a resistance to going to preschool childcare programs, particularly if they have to mix with the younger children. School age children need a very different set of play experiences.

School age children like to use real adult tools and materials. They love to cook, sew and build. They enjoy competing in real sports and responding to physical challenges. When they are tired or stressed, they need space to be alone and to curl up with a book or magazine and their own kind of music.

Choice is the key element to successful school age childcare. Without it the children will rebel and demand to stay home alone. They want the freedom to structure their own time, even though they might not yet be mature enough to do so. Getting homework done also usually necessitates some occasional or regular adult intervention.

A quality school age caregiver will ensure that your

child is both safe and involved in worthwhile activities until it is time to return home at the end of the day.

Is there any benefit to having school age children in a program?

Children who go home alone usually have to stay in behind locked doors, being careful not to let anyone know they are home alone. It is difficult to ensure that positive activities can take place in such an environment.

In a childcare program geared to the age of these children many positive things can happen. Social skills can develop and recreational and sports skills can be explored. Time can be spent outdoors without fear of having to handle difficult or frightening situations which school age children might not be prepared to handle. Children are also freed from the responsibility of having to care for younger siblings who misbehave or fight. While independence and responsibility can be learned by staying home alone, parents have to cautiously weigh the gains against what is sacrificed.

What activities should a school age program offer?

A school age program should exude a sense of organization, so that the children can understand the choices they have. Materials should be displayed with a clear indication of how and where they can be used and put away after use.

Some of the most popular activities with school age children include board games, dress-up clothes and props, art supplies, sports, building and construction sets of any kind, and music and magazines. Many of these items are the very things that they enjoyed so much as preschool children, but which they are not allowed to play with at school now. In the school age program environment, removed from younger children that might be associated with these playthings, these older children are able to again create, explore and fantasize.

When are children old enough to stay home alone?

"Self-care" is a term used to describe the time that children spend at home alone, without adult supervision. Some local jurisdictions prohibit children from being left alone, even at ten or twelve. Your local police department can tell you if any such laws are in effect in your community.

No simple test can determine if your child is ready to stay home alone. Unfortunately, many parents get pressured into making a decision based on what the child wants rather than on what they really feel. Contrary to popular belief, children who stay at home are not predominantly from low income or single parent households. Only a parent can judge a child's readiness, and this readiness is not based on age.

What are the major concerns with staying home alone?

The child's safety and mental ease are both major concerns with spending time home alone. To determine if your child can handle unlikely, but possible emergencies, ask yourself the following questions:

1. How does the child act with friends and adults?
2. Could he or she cope with the unexpected?
3. How safe is your neighborhood?
4. Are adults nearby?
5. How do you really feel?

Avoid making a decision that feels uncomfortable, or is driven by financial or work pressures. Remember that children who come home alone have to lock themselves in, cannot answer phones or doors, and cannot run outside to play. That is asking a lot of a child. Self care is never a substitute for the guidance and security of a responsible, nurturing adult who provides interesting things to do and gentle guidance and encouragement in a safe setting.

What kinds of emergencies could arise?

While everything might go just fine, a child at home alone should be prepared to deal with the unexpected. This might include hearing a noise, or feeling ill. It could also include an injury or a crank call. A method of dealing with a lost key is essential as the majority of school age children will lose their key at some time.

Rules for cooking, talking on the phone and playing with friends have to be discussed and understood before the child is ever faced with determining the limits for such situations alone. What constitutes a real emergency and a call to 911 should be clearly established, so that valuable time would not be wasted in a true emergency. And if you cannot always be reached at work, another adult's number should be available at all times.

How many school age children do stay home alone?

The cities of Los Angeles and San Diego tried to answer this question and came up with an estimate of around forty percent of their student populations under age thirteen. How close this is to the truth is anyone's guess, as most parents will not openly admit that they use self care for their children.

Are there workable solutions to the problems of self care?

If you think that your child might be able to handle short periods home alone after school, be sure to do some training for both ordinary and emergency situations, including the following:

1. Children should have their own keys. Hiding places outside the house are well known by burglars.
2. Doors should remain locked while the child is home.
3. Children should be well-trained in telephone use. This includes never letting anyone who calls know that there is no adult home.
4. Emergency numbers should be posted and children should know when to use them.
5. Rules for playing at a friend's house, cooking, and allowing playmates in the home should be agreed upon and written down.
6. Emergencies should be rehearsed ahead of time, including things like what to do in case of a stomach ache, a crank call, a noise, or a lost key.
7. Smoke alarms should be installed and properly functioning.

It should be obvious by now that handling this variety of situations will require a good deal of thinking ability and self confidence. As the parent, you are the person best equipped to make this judgment.

Where else can adolescents and teens go after school?

Adolescence is a time of transition, often accompanied by open rebellion against anything that smacks of adult direction. Lamenting that they are too old for childcare, preteens accuse parents of not trusting them when other arrangements are discussed. An even greater problem is the fact that even if you wanted care and supervision, few resources are available. Patching together a variety of occasional activities, so that the child is not home alone all the time can be a satisfactory solution. Centers for teens are rarely found, although some municipal parks and recreation departments are beginning to develop them in response to the critical need. Some have successfully combined them with senior services at community centers. Other recreation programs offer classes in sports, cooking and self-improvement, which are all popular with teens.

Another possibility is involving your child in volunteer work at hospitals, convalescent homes, food closets and preschools, for example. The yellow pages of the phone book can help you to identify organizations in the community that coordinate volunteer work. Because this is real work in the adult world, it is not only fun for teens, but also trains them in self and community responsibility. Furthermore, it provides a reference for future paid job opportunities.

Finally, many local churches offer activities specifically for teens. This can be an especially helpful resource during the summer months, when so much free time needs to be filled. Many teen activities stress values, fun and cooperation, rather than specific religious doctrine, as a means of keeping teens off the streets and out of trouble.

Special Needs Childcare

Can childcare for special needs children be found?

Information is lacking concerning the childcare needs of families with special needs children, but what we do know suggests that the need is far greater than the supply. The term "special needs" is often used interchangeably, and not necessarily correctly, with the terms exceptional needs, disabled and handicapped. Children with special needs may also include those with dietary restrictions, chronic illnesses, physical challenges and limited ability to speak English. Parents of special needs children, both preschool and elementary age, should become familiar with the community or school district services for which they are eligible.

The key in influencing childcare providers to open their regular programs to these children lies in staff training. Childcare programs often are already experiencing high staff turnover rates, and administrators might be fearful of adding another stress. Parents of special needs children can help to break down those fears by volunteering the information and expertise that staff might lack. These parents know exactly what are the needs of the child and what kind of training the caregivers need.

How does the Americans with Disabilities Act relate to childcare services?

The Americans with Disabilities Act, implemented in 1990, makes it illegal to deny childcare services to a child based on a disability. But, more importantly, it has approached the whole issue of caring for special needs children by helping childcare providers become trained in how to make simple changes in facilities and staff behaviors that will allow these children to be accepted into the mainstream.

Many providers who never cared for these children before are finding that the accommodation is not only fairly simple, but actually benefits all involved. Professional organizations in the early childhood education field are aware of the Americans with Disabilities Act, and are responding by providing appropriate training and resource materials for caregivers in nearly all communities.

Can disabled infants be successfully integrated into regular programs?

If no centers in your area are yet equipped to handle disabled infants, a college laboratory setting might be a good place to try to get one started. In this setting, training is stressed and adult to child ratios are generous. A 1992 study of integrating infants with disabilities into a regular college campus childcare program at San Diego State University found it to work quite well if certain parameters were carefully arranged. Some parameters of this successful program included:

* Student teachers who worked with both disabled and regular babies
* Training to help staff appreciate and accept differences
* Adequate respite time for staff away from all children
* Parents of both types of infants being treated exactly the same
* Sessions held for two hours, rather than full days
* Space allotments per child that were more generous than normal
* Training in both child development and special education

Because of an emerging emphasis on staff training for special needs children since ADA, a parent might do well to approach local colleges about the possibility of combining their teacher education, child development and special education training programs in some way to meet the needs of the special needs children in their community.

A resource and referral agency can also help by giving you the names of childcare centers and family childcare providers who care for special needs children. Although few caregivers have felt comfortable enough to try providing this service in the past, new training programs began since ADA are resulting in a growing number of competent and loving caregivers who serve these children.

How can a parent judge if a program will meet their child's special needs?

A quality program will meet the needs of all children enrolled by having systems in place to chart and encourage the development of each individual child. Visiting and observing a program to see if it is right for your child should leave you feeling that all of the following statements are true:

1. Each child feels loved.
2. Each child can express feelings.
3. Each child feels accepted.
4. Each child is free of fear.
5. Each child is able to act as independently as possible.
6. Each child achieves and experiences success.
7. Positive self-image is promoted.

How are specific disabilities dealt with?

If a wide range of developmentally suitable toys for the children are in the program, special needs children can use materials suited to their particular developmental stage, regardless of their chronological age. In addition to the regular toys, specifically targeted materials can be added to enhance and challenge specific groups of special needs children:

* Visually impaired — toys with texture, weight, sound and movement, large sized chalk and crayons, large paper, non-slip floors
* Hearing impaired — toys and activities with sounds and vibrations
* Physically handicapped — doors, ramps, toileting cubicles and handrails that make getting around easier, benches and step-stools by chairs and sinks
* Mentally handicapped — toys and activities that are repetitive, water-play toys, toys that appeal to many senses
* Emotionally handicapped — water-play toys, painting, books, soft cuddly toys

SCREENING PROVIDERS

Your first task in the screening process is to decide which of the four basic types of childcare mentioned in Chapter 1 best fits your needs: family home day care, childcare center, in-home care, or care by a relative. Availability of actual services in your geographical area might limit your choices, but understanding the differences will still help you to evaluate the information that you will be collecting.

Is it better to look for childcare near home or near work?

This question seems to get a great deal of attention, but it is not the most important issue. There are two general lines of thinking on this question. Parents of older children tend to want the children near home, school and the neighborhood. Parents of infants and toddlers seem to feel better if their children are closer to work during the day.

In reality, unless you come up with a fairly long list of quality program choices, you will not even have the luxury of considering location as a major criteria. The search for quality care should be your primary concern at this point. If you find quality and it turns out to be conveniently located, so much the better.

One practical consideration about location is the need to have someone available to pick-up or deliver your child if you are away, or if the child becomes injured or ill during the day. Thus it might ultimately be better to have your child located near grandma or another family member during the day.

These considerations will vary with each family situation.

If a local provider is well-known and widely used, can that be taken as a good recommendation?

If friends and neighbors have used a provider for some time, the provider is probably worth checking out. But before you accept a care situation on someone else's word, consider that some of the most notorious child abuse incidents happened in well-established, well-frequented programs. Parents accepted the programs because of their reputation. They did not question provider policies that kept adults out of the buildings. They never interviewed staff members personally and in depth. By abdicating these parental responsibilities, the children were put at risk.

You owe it to your child to go through the total search process regardless of recommendations or referrals. If you end up going back to the original provider, you can do so with a clear and informed mind, knowing that it is a good choice for your child.

Is a child's age a factor in choosing care?

Your child's age is a critical factor in choosing care. Consider the following child development milestones and be aware of them when you weigh the advantages and disadvantages of individual care situations. A more thorough examination of developmental stages of young children can be found in Appendix A.

Infants — birth to walking

Infants depend on their caregivers completely for physical and emotional needs. Infants need holding, talking and touching, and these needs must be met as consistently as possible. Basic trust is developed during this period. Growth occurs at a rapid pace so that caregivers should have specific training in infant development and an ability to anticipate the developmental needs.

Toddlers — walking to 2 or 2 ½ years

Toddlers need space and the encouragement to move and explore. Toddlers are refining their walking abilities and they are absorbing language for future endeavors in talking. They are still babies, and they need plenty of individual attention with the flexibility to adjust the day to their needs.

Preschoolers — 2 $\frac{1}{2}$ to 5 years

Preschoolers have mastered basic movement and are working on social skills and learning approaches, both of which will be vital to later school success. Preschoolers need opportunities to share, take turns, play in small groups, and follow simple directions. Imaginary play is at an all-time high, and space is needed to act out, run, jump and pretend. Bike riding, climbing, art and stories are favorite activities.

School age — 6 to 12 years

Younger school age children still need the safety and predictability of regular childcare, although they will begin to complain about going. Older children might try out a short period alone if you are sure they are mature enough for the responsibility. Caring for younger siblings is rarely advisable or appropriate for regular, long periods of time. A program for school age children should offer lots of choices and plenty of vigorous outdoor play. The time should not be used as an extension of the academic day, as these children need time to relax and unwind.

Where can parents find lists of currently operating programs?

Many people start their childcare search by scanning the phone book yellow pages. This sheer number of advertisements can quickly lead to confusion and frustration. A more productive approach might include any or all of the following strategies:

1. Call a resource and referral agency (See Appendix B).
2. Tell friends at work you are looking for childcare.
3. Talk to your neighbors.
4. Check church bulletin boards; talk to church day care coordinators.
5. Contact nanny referral agencies (See Appendix B).

Are there lists of accredited programs?

The organizations that offer accreditation procedures

to providers are listed in Appendix B. They can tell you about any programs in your area that are in the process of, or have completed accreditation. A local resource and referral agency might also have these lists.

Visiting one of these programs is a good way to get a clear idea of what quality is. Unfortunately, these programs often have long waiting lists.

How can parents find providers that offer part-time or occasional care, or care for irregular work schedules?

Many centers are happy to enroll part-time children if they have the space available. As a general rule, homes prefer full-time placements, unless they are specifically serving school age children. The number of children they serve is small and it can be difficult to match up part-time children so they can maximize income.

For evening or weekend care, a home setting is more likely to accommodate your needs. If your hours are irregular and you can afford the extra expense, it might be easier to purchase a full-time slot and use it whenever you need it.

Some strategies can be employed when bargaining with a provider to convince them to give irregular service hours. You might suggest any or all of the following:

1. Agree to give as much advance notice as possible of your work schedules.
2. Promise to call immediately if your plans change, or if your child is ill.
3. Agree on financial penalties for last minute changes.

What questions should be asked on the first screening?

Your first screening of potential providers can take place over the telephone. A form with suggested questions is included in this chapter for this task. It can be modified to incorporate any special needs or considerations you might have.

Take lots of notes as you talk so you do not have to rely on memory after you hang up. This is especially critical if you are making several phone calls at a time. Include your personal reactions to the provider's manner and tone, as well as the more factual information you will be gathering. Your goal for these calls is not to get every piece of information necessary to make a choice. You just want to screen for basic minimum requirements and get an initial feeling for programs, so that you know who merits further consideration.

The best time to telephone is after lunch, from about 1 p.m. to 2 p.m., when the children are most likely to be resting and adults can give you their full attention. Your call should be answered courteously by someone who can answer your questions or who will take your name so that your call can be returned.

If you are told that the provider is busy with the children, or if it seems noisy, don't be alarmed. While this is a business, its primary function is to care for children, not to chat with customers. If an answering machine is used, your call should be returned that day, and directions for getting through in case of an emergency should be included on the taped message.

How is telephone information evaluated and compared?

When you have contacted all of the names on your list, the calls should fall fairly readily into "Pass" and "Fail" piles. Arrange these in any priority order that you have come to during the conversations. If you end up with two to four programs that look promising, you can move on to the next stage of your search.

If you do not end up with some promising leads, don't be discouraged, as this is quite common. Gather more names and repeat the telephone process as many times as necessary. Sometimes, when you phone a resource and referral agency for names, they give out partial lists if there are many providers in a geographical area. Check to see if they have more names, and put out the word further among your friends and acquaintances.

Discard any names where the telephone response gives you a bad first impression. If you did not like a provider over the phone, there is little chance that a personal encounter will improve your feelings. This visiting stage of your search is time consuming, so you only want to invest time in visiting truly prospective leads. If you come up with more than four programs to visit, try to prioritize them into two piles, visiting the most promising ones first if you are pressed for time.

PROVIDER TELEPHONE SCREENING

Date _____ Time _____ Phone Number _____

Name of provider _____

Person spoken to _____ Title _____

Operating hours _____

Openings for my child? _____ If no, expected date _____

Total program size _____ Size of my child's group _____

Length of time in business _____

Pets or smoking _____

Fees _____

Fees charged for missed days _____

Fees charged for late pick-up _____

Other Questions _____

_____

Overall Impression _____

_____

VISITING PROGRAMS AND PROVIDERS

Visiting a childcare program can be an intimidating experience, especially if you are new to the task. The efficiency and orderliness with which a quality program operates may well feel unfamiliar to you, even if it is what you are looking for. Childcare is different than what you do at home, but keep in mind that although it may be different, it is not better. You are the expert on your child. The childcare program needs your expertise and advice to provide quality care. You can agree and disagree with how different childcare providers deliver their service, and it is within your right to do so.

Several forms are included in this chapter to help you feel more competent in your task and to assure that you get the most out of these initial visits. The first form lists the basic questions that you want to be sure to ask any provider. This is followed by supplementary forms with questions pertaining specifically to the care of infants or school age children. A series of checklists follow, for both centers and family home childcare settings, for use as you walk around and look at what is provided for the children and what the children are doing. Finally, a visit summary form is provided for use after you leave, but before you go on to the next program. Whether you feel comfortable or not as you begin this important phase of your search, these forms will help you to gather the data that you need to make a choice based on facts as well as feelings.

Should I make an appointment for my first visit?

At this exploratory stage of your search it is best to make an appointment with the program provider or director. A childcare center director or assistant director can schedule tours and interviews throughout the day, while a home childcare provider might need to limit interviews to nap time, or after work hours. You should allow an hour or more for each visit. This will include about an hour for an interview and tour, and about fifteen minutes afterward to jot down summaries of your observations and impressions.

What is the purpose of the first visit?

The first visit should focus on collecting the specific, in-depth information that you were unable to get on the phone. It is strongly recommended that you not take your child with you at this time. Not only will you be distracted, but multiple visits can confuse and upset your child. It is best not to visit more than three or four programs on any one day, as visiting is an intensive chore and impressions can begin to blur together. The more visits that you make, the more important your note-taking becomes. It is vital that your observations of each individual program remain clear and distinct.

First visits should allow you ample time to discuss basic policies with the administrator. Ask for all printed information on policies, philosophy and rules. Ask to see the basic contract and go over it in detail. When you feel you have collected all the factual information necessary, ask for a tour of the facility. Use the visual checklists to continue jotting down reactions and observations as you walk around.

After you leave, go and sit down in a quiet spot and write down conclusions on the summary form before you move on to the next program visit.

Are there some things that you should never see at a childcare program?

Certain behaviors by the adult staff are always inappropriate in a childcare setting. If you see any of these behaviors, don't waste any more time observing the program, and if you feel that the situation is serious, report what you saw to your state licensing agency or local police department. You should never witness:

* physical discipline, such as shaking or hitting
* crying children being ignored or left unattended

* young babies being fed from propped bottles
* babies left for long periods of time in cribs, high chairs, infant seats
* forced toilet training
* a child left in a wet or messy diaper for a long time
* food withheld as punishment
* belittling, ridiculing as punishment

How many times can visits be repeated?

A quality program wants parents to be comfortable and involved in the childcare experience. Actively involved parents make the transition and adjustment easier for everyone involved. Parents who visit and ask questions have fewer misunderstandings and conflicts later. Feel free to visit as many times as it takes for you to reach a comfort level. Visit with your spouse, the child's grandparents and friends. Share opinions and observations about what you see, hear and feel.

When should the child be included in the visiting process?

When you have finished visiting the programs on your list, you will have formed definite opinions about what you saw. Discuss the pros and cons of each program with your spouse, or anyone else who is helping you look for childcare. Review your notes, checklists and the summary sheets. Compare and contrast the most significant things you observed and evaluate how important they are to you. Finally, review all printed materials to see if what they say matches what you saw.

The best programs should rise to the top. If you have several good choices you will probably get down to finer issues, relating specifically to your family, in order to make a choice. Your final step will include visits with your child and reference checks. The purpose of taking your child to visit is not so much to get input, as to allow for an introduction to your probable choice. An exception to this is the school age child who can be given some voice in the decision process, but not necessarily the final say.

How can the success of the child's visit be ensured?

Unless it is a school age child, the visit should take

place in the morning, preferably between nine o'clock and eleven o'clock, as this is when the planned programming and group play that will probably be most intriguing to your child takes place. A post-nap visit in the afternoon will not be as useful, as the children will most likely be engaged in "free play" rather than in planned activities.

When visiting, encourage but do not force your child to join in the activities. Don't be concerned if your child hugs your leg and refuses to participate. This is not necessarily a negative reaction. In fact, most children need to watch for a while before joining in. Respect your child's individual style in facing this new situation.

Make positive comments about what you see, always being factual and truthful with your child. Point out menus and napping equipment so your child understands the types of activities that go on here. Give your child a chance to see and handle play materials. Get down on the child's level and talk to other children, introducing yourself and your child. Watch your child's reactions to see what is interesting or exciting.

After you leave, talk casually to your child about the visit. Try not to sound forced or anxious. Remember how good young children are at interpreting your body language and true meaning. If your child whines and complains about the visit, this might be an objection to going to childcare in general, rather than an objection to the specific program.

How should references be checked?

When considering references, always keep in mind that the reference is only as good as the person who is giving it. If you know what you want to hear before you ask, that is possibly all that you will hear. A good reference check procedure should include the following contacts:

1. If your state licenses childcare programs, call and ask if any substantiated complaints are noted in the file.
2. Ask the provider for names and phone numbers of currently enrolled parents, or ask that yours be given to other parents so that they can contact you. Keep in mind that these are names that the administrator

probably has screened for a positive feedback to you.

3. Visit the program in the early morning or late afternoon when parents are arriving and departing. Introduce yourself and ask them what they like and dislike about the provider.

4. Talk to the staff. Ask them how they like working there and how it compares to other places they have worked.

When is it time to make the choice?

If you child is showing a general hesitancy toward childcare, you might wish to make another visit, but when you are satisfied that your choice is a good one for your child, you might need to be firm and let your child know that a decision has been made. If you are making the decision without your child's consent, try to convey that his or her feelings on the decision are important.

The final chapter offers suggestions that will help you make your childcare choice work for you.

FIRST INTERVIEW QUESTIONS

Provider name_____ Date_____

Person interviewed_____ Time_____

1. What is your philosophy about caring for children?_____

_____

2. How are adult caregivers trained to carry out this philosophy?_____

_____

3. Is anyone trained in CPR and/or first aid?_____

_____

4. What discipline methods are used?_____

_____

5. Are children expected to nap? If yes, for how long?_____

_____

6. Are meals and snacks served? What nutritional guidelines are followed?

_____

7. What are the program fees? What is included? What other fees or
   penalties are there?_____

_____

8. What do you do with a child who becomes ill?_____

_____

9. Can parents make unannounced visits?_____

_____

10. How do you ensure a child's safety?_____

_____

11. How are drop-offs and pick-ups monitored?_____

_____

INFANT/TODDLER SUPPLEMENTARY QUESTIONS

Provider name_____ Date_____

Person interviewed_____ Time_____

1. What are the sleeping arrangements?

_____

2. What kind of diapers are used? Who provides them?

_____

3. What kind of food and formula do you use?

_____

4. How is information about feeding, diapering and sleeping routines
   conveyed every day?_____

_____

5. How old are the other children my child will be with? How many other
   children are there?_____

_____

6. How are staff trained?_____

_____

7. How are they scheduled? When do shift changes occur?_____

_____

8. Is there a separate outside play area?_____

_____

SCHOOL AGE PROGRAM SUPPLEMENTARY QUESTIONS

Provider name_____ Date_____

Person interviewed_____ Time_____

1. Is transportation provided to and from school?_____

_____

_____

2. Are extra activities available? (Scouts, Little League, gymnastics, etc.)
   Are there additional fees? _____

_____

_____

3. What kinds of activities can children choose from? _____

_____

_____

4. Can they choose to be indoors or outdoors?_____

_____

_____

5. Do staff have any special talents to share?_____

_____

_____

6. Is help provided for homework? _____

_____

_____

7. What kind of snack is provided?_____

_____

_____

8. How are activities geared to the individual child?_____

_____

VISUAL CHECKLIST: CENTERS
For Preschool, Infant/Toddler, and School Age

Indoor Play Areas

Play/bathroom areas clean	Y	N
Drinking water available	Y	N
Bright and pleasant	Y	N
Rooms odor free	Y	N
Individual storage space	Y	N
Individual napping equipment	Y	N
Enough play materials	Y	N
Play materials in good repair	Y	N
Stored in an orderly way	Y	N
Accessible without adult help/permission	Y	N
Art work displayed	Y	N
Activity schedule posted	Y	N
Adults can see entire room	Y	N
Places for quiet and resting	Y	N

Safety

Smoke detectors working	Y	N
Fire extinguishers current	Y	N
Electrical outlets covered	Y	N
First aid kit	Y	N
Cleaning products secured	Y	N

Caregivers

Clean and well-groomed	Y	N
Acknowledge and greet you	Y	N
Talk pleasantly to children	Y	N
Have child development training	Y	N
Experience with young children	Y	N
Manage conflicts appropriately	Y	N
Keep crying and wandering to a minimum	Y	N
Enjoy children	Y	N
Have a system for daily communication	Y	N

Outside Play Areas

Ample space to run	Y	N
Grass	Y	N
Yard, equipment in good repair	Y	N
Enough choices of activities	Y	N
Adults interacting	Y	N
Staff can see entire playground	Y	N
Sandboxes protected in a sanitary manner	Y	N

VISUAL CHECKLIST:
FAMILY HOME CHILDCARE

General Home Condition

Fire extinguisher	Y	N
Covered plug outlets	Y	N
Secured electrical cords	Y	N
Screened windows	Y	N
Evacuation plans	Y	N
Emergency drills	Y	N
Stable shelves	Y	N
No locks on bathroom doors	Y	N
Chemicals locked	Y	N
Foot stool for bathroom sink	Y	N
Knives, cooking utensils stored	Y	N

Nutrition

USDA food guidelines used	Y	N
Meals relaxed and social	Y	N

Indoor Areas

Accessible toys	Y	N
Clearly defined play areas	Y	N
Individual storage	Y	N
Places to display art and projects	Y	N
Variety of play materials	Y	N

Outdoor Areas

Fenced	Y	N
Equipment well maintained	Y	N
Garden tools stored	Y	N
Variety of age-appropriate equipment	Y	N
Swings are away from fences	Y	N

Interaction

Smiles and hugs	Y	N
Humor	Y	N
Talking to parents	Y	N
Praise and acknowledgment	Y	N

Administration

Written policies	Y	N
Current records	Y	N
Ongoing training	Y	N

CRIB SAFETY CHECKLIST

All questions should be answered "Yes".

1. Corner posts are no higher than one inch. (Corner post extensions can catch collars, bibs, necklaces and cords around the neck).

2. All side slots are in place and no more that 2 3/8 inches apart.

3. Mattress fits snugly. Not more than two fingers fit between the edge of the mattress and the crib side.

4. Paint is not old or chipped.

5. Crib toys are installed securely at both ends.

6. Crib is away from draperies or curtains with pull cords.

7. All screws, bolts and mattress supports are secure.

8. Sides are raised and secure.

9. The distance from the top of the mattress to the top of the side railing is at least 22 inches.

POST VISIT SUMMARY

Provider Name_____Date_____

Person Interviewed _____Time_____

1. Overall impression of the administrator?_____

_____

2. Were questions answered satisfactorily?_____

_____

3. Was the program clean and pleasant to be in?_____

_____

4. Were adults talking pleasantly to children, without yelling and screaming?

_____

5. Were children involved and happy?_____

_____

6. Were adults responsive to problems and difficulties?_____

_____

7. Did you feel comfortable and welcomed by all adults that you met?

_____

8. Other comments: _____

_____

_____

_____

_____

Chapter 7

MAKING IT WORK

Starting new childcare is often as difficult for the parent as for the child. Unfortunately, sensing your apprehension can make a child wonder if he or she should be worried. If you have followed the search techniques in this book, and selected your program carefully, the chances of a successful match are high. Young children really do adapt well to new situations, particularly if the important adults in their lives appear to accept the changes.

Assure your child the place you have chosen is a good place, and the people there love children. Reinforce where you will be during the day, and when you will be coming back. Since young children have a confused sense of time, try to relate it in terms of something they will be doing, like after lunch, nap, or outdoor play.

Other helpful hints:

1. Make sure your child understands that the starting day is not another visit.
2. Remind the child about who will be there and what they will be doing.
3. Let your child pick out a small toy, a stuffed animal, or a picture of you to take along.
4. Do everything you can to make mornings go smoothly.

What makes mornings go more smoothly?

Mornings cause more grief to working parents than any other time of the day, and a hectic morning almost guarantees a painful separation at childcare. The morning sets the day's tone for both of you, so careful planning and advance preparation are well worth your efforts.

This might well be the time to let all the things you swore never to do slide. Let yourself be creative! Perhaps you can learn to overlook the child who goes off in the morning happy but wearing mismatched clothes. Childcare providers are fully aware of young children's dressing patterns and won't judge you for the results. Perhaps your child would prefer breakfast in the car to a rushed breakfast at the table. The following suggestions can be used as starting points, but try anything that you think might help you all to get off to a good start:

1. Hang a calendar by your child's bed, marking childcare days clearly. Review what tomorrow is before your child goes to bed. Cross off each day at bedtime, while discussing if it is a childcare day or a stay-at-home day.
2. If your child has trouble waking up, start fifteen minutes early.
3. Buy your child an alarm clock that he or she can set.
4. Determine which routines cause the most problems and bend the rules. How about breakfast in the car? What about sleeping in sweats and wearing them in the morning, bringing a change of clothes for later?

How can separation pains be eased?

Set routines from the very beginning, and stick to them. A suggested arrival might go something like this:

1. Greet the staff and tell them about any difficulties the night before or that morning.
2. Help your child to put personal belongings away.
3. Help your child find a friend or activity or, better yet, talk about this on the way.
4. Tell your child that it is time for you to leave and when you will return.
5. Hug, kiss, leave, and don't turn around.
6. Phone the staff when you get to work if checking it makes you feel better.

What if a child is not adjusting?

Each child handles separation differently. Some wave good-bye and run to play without looking back. Others remain anxious and tearful for weeks. Children pick up on your level of stress and are fully aware of the strong effect of their whimpers and tears on you. They will not hesitate to use that power.

Wavering and bargaining are the cruelest things you can do with your child, sending a message that you doubt their ability to handle the situation, and reinforcing their fears. Stick to the routines that you have set, and phone every day, or even several times a day, until things settle down and you feel comfortable. Caregivers are used to dealing with separation anxiety, and they are pulling for you and your child's best adjustment.

What can be done to make fathers feel more comfortable in childcare settings?

Historically, fathers have not played an active role in parenting in our society, but that appears to be changing. Many fathers are assuming a far different mode of parenting than what they experienced as children. It is becoming common to see fathers alone in the grocery store or at the park with their children. Fathers are also seen more frequently delivering and picking up their children at childcare, or retrieving an ill child during the day.

Not everyone is comfortable with this new father image, and most men still feel out of place in the childcare setting. Child caregivers might also feel intimidated by fathers, as their field is largely female dominated and they might also lack role models for involved male parents. It can take a while for a comfortable level of familiarity to be achieved by everyone involved.

One of the best ways to be accepted into the childcare setting is to ask questions. Fathers can actually do this easier than many mothers, as there is a often an underlying biased belief that women come more naturally to parenting and have more factual "know-how." As women can ask for help more easily in a hardware store, so possibly can men ask for assistance in the childcare setting. Nothing brings people closer together than asking each other for help and advice.

Another way to promote a comfort level is to stay for a while when dropping off or picking up children. This means more than casual observation. It means sitting on the floor and getting to know the child's playmates. Caregivers rarely get to see their parents interacting with their children, and much can be learned on both sides from this kind of encounter.

Finally, fathers can read bulletins and parent information flyers so that they know what is going on before it happens. The paperwork that comes from childcare should be important information to both parents and caregivers gain a great deal of satisfaction from interest in the child's day and routines away from home.

What can be done with the child who balks about leaving at the end of the day?

Believe it or not, some children have just as hard a time leaving as others do arriving. Some children have trouble with both. Refusing to go home can manifest itself in a number of embarrassing (to you) behaviors such as tantrums, refusal to put away playthings, and yelling disrespectfully at you so that everyone can hear.

Some children get so deeply involved in activities that they cannot stop them abruptly. Likewise, some parents are in such a hurry to get out the door that they make the problem worse. Most children need a few minutes to disengage before making the transition to go home.

Adults who work with young children are prepared for these behaviors and can help you and your child deal with them. They have seen your child's well adjusted play behavior all day, and they know how your child reacts to transitions. They also understand how ineffective threatening and scolding are. Do not allow your child to use this as an excuse to avoid cleaning up play materials. If you need help, ask your caregiver how to handle the issue of cleaning up and then firmly, but lovingly, leave with your child.

Do mid-day visits upset children?

The frequency and timing of any daytime visits you can make depends largely on your child's age and individual personality. You should make occasional unannounced visits, regardless of your child's reactions, for safety purposes, but weigh your child's ability to understand and deal with your unexpected appearances carefully before making them a regular part of your routine.

On or near-site employer centers may have one-way viewing windows for the parents' convenience. With their use children can be viewed and enjoyed without causing unnecessary anxiety or renewed separation problems. If this is not available, or if you use a home childcare provider, make it clear to your child immediately upon your arrival that you are not coming to pick them up, but that you must return to work and will be back later.

What can be done to strengthen parent/caregiver ties?

Even though you work most of the day, you still need direct involvement in your child's day. But sometimes, parents feel like "intruders" at the childcare setting. If the caregivers are seen as the childcare experts, parents might feel uncomfortable. Sometimes parents forget that no one knows their child in the same intimate and personal way that they do. When parents feel that their parenting abilities and skills are being judged negatively, the childcare situation is less productive for everyone involved.

The idea of the parent-provider partnership goes hand in hand with the idea of quality care. In a partnership, the child is treated the same at home and at childcare, and is able to transition comfortably between the two places. When both parents and caregivers can work to provide continuity and cooperation, children thrive.

Discuss the idea of partnership with your caregiver. After all, it take two to make a partnership. As you talk, agree on some concrete ways to make your situation work for your family, your provider and your child. Here are some suggestions to help you get started:

1. Re-read all printed materials you received when you enrolled your child and ask new questions as they arise.
2. Agree that there is no such thing as a stupid question.
3. If your caregiver uses a word you are not familiar with, ask for a definition.
4. Read all newsletters and parent bulletin boards regularly.
5. Attend potlucks, parent nights, and holiday programs.
6. Allow time every day to find out how your child's day went.
7. Sit on the floor, or at the child-sized tables, and watch your child play, showing that you are

comfortable there.

8. Try to appear unhurried as you come and go, so your caregivers can share anecdotes to you about your child.
9. Respond to all written communications that are sent home.
10. Provide plenty of extra clothing, clearly marked with your child's name.
11. Offer to take home little projects once and a while, like cutting out materials, mending doll clothes or repairing torn books.
12. Remember your child's caregiver on his or her birthday, on holidays and just to say "thank you".

How do working parents deal with all there is to do?

No one would argue that working parents have incredibly busy lives. Sorting out priorities on a regular basis is an ongoing task that effects how well you adapt to changes. This means that sometimes a child who needs to be held comes before folding the laundry or emptying the dishwasher. This can also mean redefining just what a clean house is at this point in life.

Try to look realistically at meal preparation, outside volunteer work and other family obligations, understanding that this is a time of your life when you just cannot have it all. Tackle some of the more obvious, but often overlooked areas you can focus on:

1. Help your children understand what you do. Even at age three or four, a child can understand that daddy teaches school, and mommy works on a computer.
2. Don't overwork; children resent it when you regularly bring work home, and they are told to be quiet or go outside.
3. Try not to come home grumpy, because of something that happened at work.
4. Keep evening meetings and social events to a minimum as children need your regular presence in the evening.
5. Start the day with good, workable routines that everyone agrees with, and follow them with a hug and kiss.

6. Divide household chores with your spouse or other household members.

Does childcare add to, or alleviate, stress?

Finding quality childcare does not mean that the battle is over. Internal doubts and questions will continue, particularly if your child is very young. It is normal to worry if your child is all right when you are gone; whether he or she is worried or scared; whether your child will remember that you are the parent. It is natural to feel that no one can care for your child like you do. In many ways, you are correct. Parent care may well be the best care, but quality care outside of the family is possible. Your child has the ability to adapt to other caregivers and to thrive in other situations.

As young children grow, their needs and schedules change frequently. Such changes have nothing to do with a loss of control on your part. Your own busy schedule is not the cause for the changes that occur. Children do get sick, miss naps and occasionally need more attention in order to cope. As you and the caregiver recognize these changes and communicate them to each other, you will both be able to accept the changes and deal with them more naturally.

Be realistic in your own expectations about being a parent and about the amount of time you intend to spend with your child, especially at the end of the day. If you look forward all day to spending intimate time together from 6 p.m. to 7 p.m., and your child falls asleep, it is easy to feel like you have failed. Perhaps falling asleep in your comforting arms is just as good or even better than what you had planned. Any time spent holding or talking to your child is quality time, and sometimes you just have to catch it as it flies by.

Do extremely active children adjust to childcare?

Highly active children present a special challenge to group childcare settings. Usually bright and creative, they often exhibit a tendency to take risks and ignore possible consequences. These are great attributes — later in life! For preschool children it is normal for attention spans to vary from seconds to several minutes. Only when attention spans are brief for all situations is there cause for concern.

Although sustained attention and focus is necessary in elementary school, it is not as relevant in preschool children whose immediate interests, health conditions, and moods can override their efforts at concentration.

Discuss your child's energy level candidly with the caregiver so that plans can be made to help your child adapt successfully. Routines are important for active children. They may have a difficult time starting and stopping activities and working in groups, so that gentle, patient adult direction is needed. Rules should be discussed and limitations clearly understood, with the child knowing that you and the caregiver have regular open communications. Be sure that you are both focusing on positive things that the child does during the day, rather than what might be perceived as problems.

How can parents plan ahead for the inevitable sick days?

All young children become ill from time to time, causing a great deal of anxiety for their working parents. How your caregiver deals with this varies widely and needs to be discussed before the inevitable event happens. In some states it is illegal to keep sick children in the same facility as children who are healthy. Within the family childcare system, the decision to keep ill children is generally up to the provider. If you are faced with finding a back-up plan, here are some ways that other parents cope:

1. Split the day so each spouse stays home half-time.
2. Use a relative as a back-up plan for emergency care or to pick up a sick child at childcare. Remember to have this person listed on your emergency card.
3. Contact local churches and see is anyone provides emergency sick care for working parents.
4. Call a resource and referral agency to find out who provides sick childcare in your community.
5. Talk to your boss about taking work home when occasional sickness occurs.
6. Call nanny agencies listed in the yellow pages of the phone book to locate services. Remember that these services might be more costly than your regular childcare.

If you will need to leave your child with another adult, arrange for this before an illness happens. It is probably wise to make sure that your child meets this person and understands what the procedures will be. Always leave written detailed instructions and keep them in a folder, ready for use.

Are there things that a child should never bring to childcare?

It is never appropriate to send the following items to childcare. If you do, they will probably be taken away and returned to you at the end of the day, causing your child unnecessary grief:

* toy guns
* gum or candy
* expensive or fragile toys
* anything of a sentimental or monetary value

How should children be dressed?

Resist the temptation to have the best dressed child in the group. Children cannot engage in vigorous, creative play in their best clothes. Remember that if children do all the things that they need to grow and develop, they should come home looking quite different than they did when they arrived in the morning.

Send your child in durable, washable play clothes with as few buttons and zippers as possible. Elastic is always easier for little hands to pull on and off, increasing independent behavior. All children have favorite clothes, but they should be worn only if they do not hinder the activities they enjoy doing.

Can birthdays be celebrated?

Celebrating a birthday with friends is special to a young child. Find out how your child's caregiver prefers to handle birthdays and follow with those guidelines. Limits on sugar and party favors will probably be recommended. Infants and toddlers should never be offered frosted cake or candy, as many cannot tolerate large amounts of sugar. A cereal based cookie is usually preferable, and makes cleanup easier.

Can a child with a cold be kept inside?

When children are not sick enough to stay home, but

are not quite at their physical best, it is tempting to ask that they be kept indoors. Actually, more germs are passed in a closed, heated room than outside in the fresh air. Your caregiver might not be able to supervise a child indoors while others are playing outside, and your request might depend on the availability of another adult to remain indoors and supervise your child. At the least, you can insist that your child wear a jacket for outdoor play.

What happens to fussy eaters?

If your caregiver provides meals and your child is a picky eater, you could have an issue that needs to be addressed. Tell your caregiver about your child's eating preferences and make sure that there is not a policy forcing children to try to eat every food served. Breakfast and lunch menus should include fruit and milk or juice, and if eaten along with an afternoon snack, can get your child through the day even if the main course is refused.

If you are allowed to send food from home when a menu item causes a problem, remember that sweet or snack foods are inappropriate in a setting where nutritious eating habits are being established.

Never try to bargain with a reluctant child by slipping them a pack of gum or candy at separation time. Most programs will simply confiscate such items and return them to you at the end of the day. This will be more upsetting to your child in the long run.

Are prayers said at meals or at other times?

Programs or caregivers should not teach children prayers or rhymes of a religious nature. If you would like your child to say prayers, investigate a church or religious-oriented childcare provider.

Problems sometimes arise during the holiday season, although many programs make a concerted effort not to focus on any one religious tradition. Sharing Sunday school experiences is an area in which a child's excitement cannot be invalidated, although there is no need to dwell on the subject matter. To convey to a child that their excitement about a religious book or activity is inappropriate would be confusing and unfair to a child, but so would an in-depth discussion with the group as a whole. Never send religious story books to share, even if they are your child's favorite.

When should a parent consider changing childcare?

One of your main objectives in choosing childcare is to ensure stability. Frequent changes are disruptive, both to you and to your child. But while changes should never be made lightly, there are times when there is no other alternative. Caregivers move and go out of business, and what can start out looking like the perfect place can prove to be otherwise. Multiple changes can be harmful, especially for infants and toddlers, which reinforces the necessity for choosing carefully in the first place. However, children are amazingly resilient if they sense from you that a change is coming and should be accepted.

If you have to change caregivers, take precautionary steps to help your child transition more easily:

1. Never criticize or argue with the caregiver in front of your child, no matter how strong your negative feelings.
2. Be clear with your child about when the last day will be. Give ample forewarning.
3. Be prepared for tears and acting out. Don't stifle your child's emotions or feelings.
4. Visit the new caregiver as many times as practical.
5. Take pictures of your child with best friends before leaving.
6. Send a going-away snack for a small farewell party.
7. After the move, pay attention to your child's feelings, encouraging expression of them.

Withdraw from your childcare immediately if you ever think that your child's safety or well-being has been threatened, and notify authorities.

What are the most common signs of child abuse?

Because of their powerless positions, children can be vulnerable to abuse by adults who care for them. Any single indicator listed below does not mean that child abuse has occurred, but should cause you to be alert and inquisitive. If several of the indicators occur, and are consistent or extreme, action should be taken immediately to withdraw the child and report the details to the police:

Physical signs

* unusual bruises or welts
* burns
* frequent urinary infections
* pain with urination
* vaginal or rectal bleeding
* swollen genitals
* torn or stained underwear

Behavioral signs

* clinging
* apprehension
* fear of the caregiver
* sudden, extreme reluctance to go to childcare
* sleep disorders
* bed-wetting
* return to thumb-sucking
* mature interest in sexual behaviors

Do employers have a role in helping working parents deal with childcare issues?

Over the past ten years more employers implemented benefits and policies to assist their employees deal with family issues. This is seen as a way of stabilizing the workforce, reducing absenteeism, and increasing job satisfaction and productivity. Workers who are confident that their children are being well cared for are better able to concentrate on the jobs.

Assistance takes many forms, with on-site childcare being the most visible. However, childcare centers are not the most frequently chosen benefit, nor are they necessarily the most cost-effective.

How can I approach my employer about doing something for the working parents at my job?

For many parents, 5 p.m. is just the beginning of the next shift; racing to ball practice, the orthodontist, or meetings, and tending to necessary chores like cooking, laundry and housework. Many employers are starting to recognize that what goes on at home affects what goes on at the workplace. This realization often begins with requests from employees who make their needs known to their employer either individually or in groups.

If you approach your employer, do not be surprised if there is not as positive a reception to your ideas as you might wish. Many employers find the link between family benefits and the bottom line to be tenuous at best. It can be a slow process to replace uncertainty with facts about success stories.

What kinds of things can employers do for their workers?

Benefits to address work/family issues must be customized to the company if they are to be truly useful. The same solutions will not work for everyone, and expectations should not be raised higher that can be reasonably satisfied.

Most companies have neither the population nor the resources to open a childcare center, but they can still offer meaningful assistance to the employees through some of these other programs:

Dependent Care Assistance Plan (DCAP)
Under IRS Code 129, employees can elect to have money set aside from their earnings before taxes are deducted, in order to pay for a portion of their childcare expenses.

Vendor
An employer can purchase childcare spaces from a local childcare provider for its own employees.

Voucher
An employer can issue vouchers that can be used to pay for the childcare services of the parent's choice. In some states, this contribution can be claimed as an employer tax credit.

Resource and referral
A contract can be set up with a local resource and referral agency to provide services directly to company employees who are looking for childcare.

Alternate Work Schedules

Personnel policies can allow employees new work options like flextime, telecommuting, job-sharing and permanent part-time schedules to accommodate childcare responsibilities.

Parent education

Materials and presentation can be made at the worksite on a wide range of parenting issues. The content should come from the interests and needs of the actual participants. A sample Parent Interest Survey for use in documenting interests is found in Appendix A.

What kinds of companies have their own childcare centers?

Employers, both large and mid-sized, build childcare centers when they feel there will be a direct payback in lower absenteeism and reduced turnover. Some state offer tax incentives for employers who wish to undertake either the building or renovation of a building for a childcare program. A list of some of the current operating employer-supported childcare centers around the country can be found in Appendix B.

What if parents prefer a home childcare setting?

Some new models of employer supported home childcare networks are also beginning to appear. One notable system of collaboration is operating in the city of Ventura, California, in which private companies, the city and the county have set up a network of more than thirty homes to serve their employers. A contact for this program is listed in Appendix B under Successful Employer Childcare Models.

Where can I find out what employers in my area are doing?

A resource and referral agency is a good place to start finding out what other local companies are doing, and what resources are available in your community. Volunteer to organize an employee study group to gather information and ideas from fellow employees. Be sure to make it clear that your group is not asking for an expensive childcare center, but just a chance to look at the wide range of possibilities to see what might meet people's needs.

Start small and ask for the free or low cost options like lunchtime educational parenting workshops. Build your group and knowledge from there, communicating regularly with your manager or human resource director. Volunteer to help your human resource department perform an employee needs assessment to find out what the most common issues and concerns really are.

How can local government help with childcare?

Today's children are tomorrow's leaders, and most American cities are experiencing an upsurge of destructive, anti-social behaviors from their young people. Improving the conditions of the children in all communities is a real government priority. Consider how many local government departments in your municipality directly affect children and childcare:

Economic development — Luring new jobs into the community means creating greater needs for childcare services.

Recreation — Besides parks and golf courses, services can be provided like tiny tots, after school programs, and summer youth employment.

Health — Assistance is provided with required immunizations and disease control.

Planning and zoning — Regulations are determined that will directly affect the ability to open new childcare programs.

Police — Support is offered through community awareness education, safety programs, and abuse and neglect investigation.

Fire — Support is offered to ensure the safety of children in major emergencies or natural disasters.

City Hall — Offices of Child Care Assistance/ Coordination are appearing throughout the country to bring community resources together to meet local needs.

What can parents do to assure that all children get quality childcare?

Parents are often the missing link in child advocacy in

Washington, D.C., and in state capitols. Even if you have never written a letter or made a phone call to an elected official, it is never too late to get started. Your own personal childcare stories and anecdotes are exactly what legislators need to hear. This is the material that they quote in their testimony. Try using one of the issues below to get started. Look up your legislator's address in the governmental pages at the beginning of the phone book. Tell your legislator what you think and ask them to tell you their views in response.

1. Talk about your community. Is there enough childcare? School age childcare? Infant childcare?
2. Talk about your childcare costs. How much of your total income goes towards childcare?
3. What kind of people take care of your children? How much do they make? Have they ever considered leaving the field because of low wages and inadequate benefits?
4. How do you feel about the way the country or your state deals with childcare issues? Is funding a priority? Are there laws to protect children?
5. Is there support for childcare from the business community? Would tax incentives help?

Your choice in selecting a childcare provider should serve your needs and those of your child well into the future. Finding good care is only part of the task, and with a little luck and a great deal of work, you will not have to repeat the search process for a long time.

Appendix A

SAMPLE DOCUMENTS
USDA GUIDELINES
DEVELOPMENTAL MILESTONES

CHILDCARE REGISTRATION CONTRACT

Child's Name_____

Date of Admission _____

I agree that:

1. My child will be attending

Days_____

Hours_____

2. My fees will be $_____, for the period_____to_____, due on _____, or I will pay a late-fee of_____.

3. The program hours are_____to_____, and I will pick up my child by_____each day.

4. If I cannot pick up my child, a person designated and authorized by me will do so.

5. I will pay a late pick-up fee of _____for each_____minutes that I am late.

6. My registration fee of_____is non-refundable.

7. There is no credit for absence, or days missed.

8. My child will not be sent ill, and I will pick him/her up should illness occur during the day.

9. My child will have a current T.B. test and physical examination on file.

10. I will sign a medication form for any medicine that is to be administered to my child during the day.

11. I will sign my child in and out each day.

12. I will give_____days notice if I withdraw from the program.

13. The following meals and snacks will be provided during the day:
_____

14. The center is closed on the following holidays:_____
_____
_____

15. Other conditions: _____
_____
_____

signed_____date_____

CONSENT FOR EMERGENCY MEDICAL CARE

I,_____
_____ mother _____ father _____ guardian

hereby give my consent to _____
who will be caring for my child _____
born on _____
for the period _____ to _____
to arrange for emergency medical/surgical/dental care and treatment
(including diagnostic procedures) necessary to preserve the health of my
child. I acknowledge that I am responsible for all reasonable charges in
connection with any care or treatment rendered.

Print name_____ Pediatrician_____

_____   _____

Home address_____ Address_____

_____   _____

_____   _____

Home telephone_____ Telephone_____

Work telephone_____

Name and address of health insurance carrier:_____

_____

_____

_____

Group Number_____

Allergies_____
Chronic illnesses_____
Last tetanus booster_____
Current medications_____

Signature_____Date_____

INFANT/TODDLER DAILY RECORD

Child's Name_____Date_____
Caregiver's Name_____

Entrance Health Screening:
_____completed with no unusual findings
_____completed with the following findings_____
_____

Feedings and amounts before arrival:
Breakfast_____
Lunch_____
Snacks_____

Sleep and naps before arrival_____

Diaperings at childcare
Bowel movement times   _____ _____ _____ _____ _____
Diaper change times   _____ _____ _____ _____ _____

General comments: _____
_____
_____
_____
_____

INJURY REPORT

Name of Child_____

Injury_____
_____
_____

Time of Injury_____

Name of Parent/Guardian_____

Notified_____

Action Taken_____
_____

By_____

Who observed accident_____
Comments_____

SAMPLE PROGRAM PHILOSOPHY

Infant/Toddler Program

The Infant/Toddler Program is designed for children ranging from six weeks to twenty-four months. Caregivers are trained to accommodate the special needs of very young children using the following developmental principles:

1. Children are allowed to develop at their own natural level. All sleeping and eating routines are to be strictly individual, based on each child unique needs.

2. The environment will be safe and secure, promoting exploration, movement and curiosity. Children will begin to learn to make choices, to express emotions, to develop independence, and to learn about other people and cultures.

3. Activities will be offered which stimulate sensory motor development, language development and social interaction.

4. Discipline will never be a part of the Infant/Toddler Program.

Preschool Program

The Preschool Program serves children from two to five years of age and is available in both morning and full day sessions. The preschool experience involves both the parents and staff in planning to meet the needs of each child. Ideals of peace, love, respect and creativity will be nurtured throughout the curriculum.

In assisting each child to develop to full potential, the program will strive to encourage physical, intellectual, social and emotional growth. The development of strong self-esteem is also a major goal. These goals are accomplished by:

Offering a large choice of experiences
Developing listening and speaking skills
Providing play experience alone and in groups
Stimulating curiosity
Teaching responsibility for one's own actions

School Age Program

The School Age Program operates on the belief that elementary school children have needs far different from the children in the Preschool Program. The School Age Program is based on the ability of the child to make, plan and execute individual and group activities. A wide range of indoor and outdoor materials are available to allow children a full range of choice and expression.

Homework is between the parent, teacher and child. It is the child's responsibility to acknowledge assignments and to utilize the homework time/area available in the after-school program. A supervised homework time is available for those who wish to do homework assignments before going home. Adults will be available to assist with questions and tutoring.

The children will be expected to respect the staff, each other and their facility in order to maintain a positive atmosphere.

DAILY SCHEDULE

Infant/Toddler Program

6:00-8:30	Greetings; breakfast for those who have not eaten
8:30-9:00	Diapering
9:00-10:30	Free play — indoors or outdoors; morning naps
10:30-11:00	Snack; diapering
11:00-1:00	Free play; lunch
1:00-1:30	Clean up; diapering
1:30-3:30	Nap; free play — indoors or outdoors
3:30-4:00	Diapering
4:00-600	Free play; snack

Free play includes stories, music, walks outdoors, ball play, water play, etc.

Preschool Program

6:30-8:30	Indoor social play activities
8:00-8:30	Breakfast is offered
8:00-8:45	Choice of outdoor play activities
8:45-9:00	Morning greeting
9:00-9:20	Circle Time
9:20-9:55	Choice of indoor guided projects
9:55-10:00	Transition
10:00-10:15	Morning snack
10:15-10:50	Outdoor play
10:50-11:00	Transition
11:00-11:45	Art and social play
11:45-12:00	Clean up for lunch
12:00-12:30	Lunch
12:30-12:50	Cleanup, toileting, nap preparation
12:50-2:30	Nap
2:30-2:45	Transition
2:45-3:30	Outdoor play
3:30-3:45	Snack
3:45-5:00	Choice of indoor/outdoor play
5:00-6:00	Story time and quiet activities indoors

School Age Program

Morning

6:30—8:00	Breakfast; indoor free play
8:00—9:00	Students leave for school, as scheduled

Afternoon

2:30—3:00	Children return from school
3:00—3:30	Prepare and eat snack
3:30—4:00	Supervised homework
4:00—6:00	Free play indoors or outdoors

Family Home Childcare

6:00—8:00	Greetings; breakfast; clean-up
8:00—9:00	Free play — indoors or outdoors
9:00—11:00	Planned play activities; errands; snack
11:00—11:30	Clean up; prepare for lunch
11:30—12:30	Lunch; clean up
12:30—1:00	Outdoor play
1:00—3:00	Nap
3:00—3:30	Wake-up; snack
3:30—5:00	Free play and planned activities
5:00—6:00	Quiet activities; prepare to go home

Note: due to mixed ages, feedings and naps are adjusted to individual children.

SURVEY OF PARENT INTERESTS

Select the five areas of greatest concern or interest and list them in order of importance.

_____ Coping with household tasks
_____ Coping with parenting responsibilities
_____ Ability to discipline
_____ Satisfaction with parenting skills
_____ Ability to spend sufficient quality time with family
_____ Satisfaction with childcare
_____ Interactions with childcare provider
_____ Knowledge of basic child development
_____ Having time to yourself

Other_____

_____

_____

_____

_____

_____

UNITED STATES DEPARTMENT OF AGRICULTURE FOOD GUIDELINES FOR CHILDREN

Recommended Daily Allowances by Age

Breakfast

Type of food	1-3 years	3-6 years	6-12 years
milk	1/2 cup	3/4 cup	1 cup
vegetable/fruit	1/4 cup	1/2 cup	1/2 cup
bread	1/2 slice	1/2 slice	1 slice
grain	1/4 cup	1/4 cup	1/2 cup

Lunch/Supper

Type of food	1-3 years	3-6 years	6-12 years
milk	1/2 cup	3/4 cup	1 cup
vegetable/fruit,	1/4 cup	1/2 cup	3/4 cup
bread	1/2 slice	1/2 slice	1 slice
grain	1/4 cup	1/4 cup	1/2 cup
meat/meat alternate	1 oz.	1 1/2 oz.	2 oz.

Snacks

Type of food (choose two types)	1-3 years	3-6 years	6-12 years
milk	1/2 cup	1/2 cup	1 cup
vegetable/fruit	1/2 cup	1/2 cup	3/4 cup
bread	1/2 slice	1/2 slice	1 slice
grain	1/4 cup	1/4 cup	1/2 cup
Meat/meat alternatives	1/2 oz.	1/2 oz.	1 oz.

DEVELOPMENTAL STAGES OF CHILDREN

Each child is an individual and develops at his and her own rate, but knowing the basic developmental milestones can help the parent and provider judge if the care and play materials are developmentally appropriate for the child.

1 Month
Not able to support own head. Alert about one hour in every ten. Needs food, warmth, handling and kisses.

3 Months
Plays with hands and feet. Laughs and coos. Needs a view of the world from a stroller, or from a lap.

Caregiver challenges: providing basic comfort and stability through timely response to basic needs, rocking, stroking, smiling, talking and eye contact.

5-6 Months
Rolls over and sits with support. Holds own toys. Alert for two-hour stretches. Eats baby food. Needs good nutrition, safety with new explorations and a change of scenery.

Caregiver challenges: keeping infants busy with the right playthings, and by providing conversation and interaction.

9 Months
Crawls, sits up and grabs. Understands simple commands. Busy! Needs locks on cabinets, fresh air, sand, water and swings.

Caregiver challenges: allowing for an emotional attachment; respect for the inborn temperament and personality. Providing play materials and room to move.

12 Months
Curious and into everything. Needs someone for slow walks. Needs freedom with someone near to help out.

Caregiver Challenges: Providing toys with moving parts, encouragement with words and language, interesting experiences, cuddling and love.

12-18 Months

Insists on self-feeding, exploring high and low, having own way (tantrums), acting fearful and clingy. Likes crayons, routines, music, imitating gestures and words, balls, sand and dirt, saying, "No".

Caregiver challenges: Allowing and encouraging safe exploration. Being patient and understanding. Getting down on eye level. Offering enough experiences to keep child from being bored. Keeping eating routines pleasant.

18-36 Months

A time of "scientific" discovery to find out how the world works. Egocentric, understanding only own experiences. Insists on hurrying, trying to explain with words, using imagination, repeating things over and over again, demanding and refusing. Likes imitating and pretending, watching and playing beside other children (not with them), having help dealing with fears, talking to oneself.

Caregiver Challenges: Providing routines that are secure and predictable. Praising accomplishments. Being patient with emotional outbursts and sudden, easy fright. Planning ahead and communicating what is planned.

3 Years

Beginning imaginary play. A positive stage, that is learning to share and be more cooperative. Can dress and self-feed. Listens and can be reasoned with. Learning to use words instead of crying, pushing or grabbing. Often becomes toilet trained.

Caregiver challenges: Encourage the use of words to have needs met. Including new and novel experiences. Encouraging some cooperative play. Encouraging self-help skills.

4 Years

A very physically active stage with lots of running, jumping and climbing. Asks unlimited questions. Learning about numbers and letters; loves to be read to. Friends are very important. Speaks clearly and like to rhyme and play with language.

Caregiver challenges: Providing sufficient vigorous play activities. Encouraging a love of reading and language. Taking time to listen and to praise.

5 Years
Growth is slowing down. Good moving skills and improving hand-eye coordination. Able to do more group activities and to concentrate and focus longer. Improved memory. Like to please adults.

Caregiver Challenges: Allowing room to explore and test out limits. Following firm and consistent rules and enforcement. Offering a good variety of play materials and experiences. Reading, talking and listening. Providing security, love and affection, especially when things fall apart.

6-7 Years
Most enter school eagerly. Still self-centered and demanding at times. Cannot wait, but move slowly themselves. Beginning to prefer same-gender friends, unless play is set up to include both sexes. Play well in groups.

Caregiver challenges: Providing stimulating materials and experiences. Encouraging use of words to settle problems. Challenging creativity and imagination.

8 Years
Curious and eager. Play with friends is the most important part of the day. Interested in the adult world and in what their parents do.

Caregiver Challenges: Being good listeners. Keeping promises. Expecting conflicts; helping children to work them out verbally. Setting and enforcing rules consistently. Expecting accidents from risk-taking and experimentation.

9-12 Years
Called "middle childhood," this is a time of power and independence. Often overly concerned with growing up faster. Some signs of puberty begin to appear, although not in all children. Girls grow more than boys. An abundance of energy and a love of organized team sports is the major highlight. Greater mental powers exhibit themselves in collecting, interests in new skills, handling money, playing games and keeping scores and justice.

Caregiver challenges: Being and acting what is preached. Keeping promises. Providing enough physical play/

activities. Allowing argument; letting children work things out whenever possible. Fostering idealism and hope. Listening and taking concerns seriously.

Appendix   B

RESOURCES

American Association of University Women
2401 Virginia Ave., NW
Washington, D.C. 20037
Tracks many work/family programs; has projects on childcare and elder care.

Au Pair/Homestay USA
World Learning Inc.
1015 15th St. NW, Suite 750
Washington, D.C. 20005
Screens caregivers from other countries who will provide childcare in exchange for living with a family in the United States.

Au Pair in America
The American Institute for Foreign Study
102 Greenwich Ave.
Greenwich, CT 06830
Screens caregivers from other countries who will provide childcare in exchange for living with a family in the United States.

Bureau of National Affairs, Work and Family Programs
1231 25th Street, NW
Washington, D.C. 20037
Maintains a database on currently operating employer-supported childcare projects.

Child Care Action Campaign
330 Seventh Ave., 18th Floor
New York, N.Y. 10001
An information gathering and advocacy organization on issues of childcare on the national level.

Child Care Law Center
22 Second Street
San Francisco, CA 94105
Publishes information on a wide array of legal issues relating to childcare including insurance, tax provisions, model dependent care assistance programs, childcare centers, tax credits, licensing, contracts, nonprofit status, and school age childcare.

Children's Defense Fund
122 C Street, NW
Washington, D.C. 20001
A national advocacy organization dedicated to children's issues. Provides information on what states are doing to encourage employer-sponsored programs, and on state and federal legislation affecting childcare. Produces an annual "State Child Care Fact Book."

Consumer Product Safety Commission
Washington, D.C. 20207
800-638-2772
A resource for checking on the safety of play equipment and children's furnishings.

Cooperative Extension Services
U.S. Department of Agriculture
Room 3444, South Building
Washington, D.C. 20250-0900
202-447-2018
Assistance with starting cooperative childcare ventures and childcare networks.

Family Child Care Project
Wheelock College, Center for Policy and Training
200 The Riverway
Boston, MA 02215
617-734-5200, ext. 291
Assistance with cooperative childcare ventures and networks, especially for school age childcare.

International Nanny Association
P.O Box 26522
Austin, TX 75755
Publishes a state-by-state directory of placement agencies that specialize in helping parents to find live-in care for their children.

National Association of Child Care Resource and Referral Agencies
2116 Campus Dr., SE
Rochester, ME 55904
800-462-1660
Maintains a list of resource and referral agencies throughout the United States.

National Association for the Education of Young Children (NAEYC)
1509 16th Street, NW
Washington, D.C. 20036
800-424-2460
The main national professional organization for persons working with young children in childcare programs. Also operates the NAEYC childcare center accreditation project and maintains lists of accredited programs.

National Association for Family Child Care (NAFCC)
725 15th Street, NW, Suite 505
Washington, D.C. 20005
202-347-3356
Maintains lists of local family childcare associations. Provides professional information and training to family home day care providers.

National Association of Hospital Affiliated Child Care Programs
9100 W. 74th Street
Shawnee Mission, KS 66201
Maintains a list of member hospital organizations that provide childcare services for their employees.

National Center for Nutrition
216 West Jackson Blvd., #800
Chicago, IL 60606
A resource for questions on child nutrition and diet.

National Center for the Prevention of Sudden Infant Death Syndrome
800-638-SIDS
National information and support group for families who have experienced the death of a young child.

National Cooperative Bank
1630 Connecticut Ave. NW
Washington, D.C. 20007
Financing for the start-up of cooperative childcare programs.

National Council of Jewish Women
53 West 23rd Street
New York, N.Y. 10010
212-645-4048
Issues study papers and findings relating to all types of childcare. Has developed materials specific to family home childcare and home childcare networks.

National Health Information Clearinghouse
U.S. Office of Disease Prevention and Health Promotion
800-336-4797
Answers questions relating to child health and welfare.

National League of Cities
1303 Pennsylvania Ave., NW
Washington, D.C. 20004
202-626-3000
Addresses issues of childcare on the city/governmental level.

School Age Child Care Project
Wellesley College Center for Research on Women
Wellesley, MA 02181
Provides technical assistance, information and written materials for those operating or wishing to start a school age program.

Sesame Street Preschool Education Program
Children's Television Network
One Lincoln Plaza
New York, N.Y. 10023

United States Department of Agriculture
Washington, D.C. 20250-0900
*Publishes nutritional guidelines, menus and other nutritional
publications.*

SAMPLES OF SELECTED EMPLOYER-SUPPORTED CHILDCARE PROGRAMS

America West Airlines
Summa Associates
735 E. Guadalupe Road
Tempe, AZ 85283

Apple Computer
20525 Mariani
Cupertino, CA 95014

Genentech, Inc.
460 Point San Bruno Blvd.
S. San Francisco, CA 94080

Mount Carmel Mercy Hospital Child Care Center
17330 Schaefer
Detroit, MI 48235

Polaroid Corporation
Community Relations Division
549 Technology Square
Cambridge, MA 02139

Proctor and Gamble
1 Proctor and Gamble Plaza
Cincinnati, OH 45202

Stride Rite Children's Center
5 Cambridge Center
Cambridge, MA 02142

Syntex Corporation
3401 Hillview Ave.
Palo Alto, CA 94304

World Bank Children's Center
H1000, 1818 H Street, NW
Washington, D.C. 20433

Ventura County Child Care Cooperative Network
Child Care Coordinator
Ventura County
800 W. Victoria
Ventura, CA 93009

Bibliography

Accreditation Criteria and Procedures of the National Academy of Early Childhood Programs, NAEYC, 1991, Washington, D.C.

Caring For America's Children, Annes Meadows, Ed., National Research Council, 1991, Washington D.C.

Child Care: A Workforce Issue, U.S. Department of Labor, 1988, 200 Constitution Ave., NW, Washington, D.C.

Child Care: The Bottom Line, Child Care Action Campaign, 1988, New York, N.Y.

Child Care Center Legal Handbook, Child Care Law Center, 1987, San Francisco, CA.

Corporate Reference Guide to Work-Family Programs, Galinsky, Friedman, and Hernandez, Work/Family Institute, 1992, New York, N.Y.

The Demand and Supply of Child Care in 1990, Willer, Hofferth, Kisker, Divine-Hawkins, Farquhar, Glantz, NAEYC, 1991, Washington, D.C.

Employers and Family Day Care, Ward, National Council of Jewish Women, 1991, New York, N.Y.

Family Day Care: Out of the Shadows and into the Limelight, Kontos, Ed., NAEYC, 1992, Washington, D.C.

Hospital Sponsored Child Care: A 1988 National Study, American College of Healthcare Executives, 1989, Melrose Park, IL.

Linking Work-Family Issues to the Bottom Line, Friedman, The Conference Board Report, No. 962, 1991, New York, N.Y.

Not Too Small to Care: Small Businesses and Child Care, Eichman and Reisman, Child Care Action Campaign, 1991, New York, N.Y.

Strategies for Promoting a Work-Family Agenda, Friedman, Johnson, The Conference Board Report, No. 973, 1991, New York, N.Y.

Who Cares for America's Children?, Hayes, Palmer, Zaslow, Eds., National Academy Press, 1990, Washington, D.C.